C000154118

THE BUSINESS

— OF —

FREEDOM

How to **escape** employment and
build a business that works for you

LISA ZEVI

Rethink

First published in Great Britain in 2022
by Rethink Press (www.rethinkpress.com)

© Copyright Lisa Zevi

All rights reserved. No part of this publication may be reproduced, stored in or introduced into a retrieval system, or transmitted, in any form, or by any means (electronic, mechanical, photocopying, recording or otherwise) without the prior written permission of the publisher.

The right of Lisa Zevi to be identified as the author of this work has been asserted by her in accordance with the Copyright, Designs and Patents Act 1988.

This book is sold subject to the condition that it shall not, by way of trade or otherwise, be lent, resold, hired out, or otherwise circulated without the publisher's prior consent in any form of binding or cover other than that in which it is published and without a similar condition including this condition being imposed on the subsequent purchaser.

Praise

'This book makes jumping off that cliff not such a lonely journey. It's only as isolating as you want it to be and reminds me that there are many people out there doing the same.'
— **Marisa Shek**, Director at Shek Architects

'Lisa Zevi's book is a wonderfully sensitive and valuable guide to those thinking of transitioning from the corporate track to a more entrepreneurial path. But it is more than that. It also helps those who have already taken that journey to identify where improvements can be made to their fledgling, or already successful, new business. Highly recommended…'
— **Charles Rustin**, Chief Growth Officer at NextWave Consulting

'Lisa gives the reader a wonderful structure to aid making a great career and life choice. The reader self-reflects their own deepest desires and fears which frame the circumstances they currently find themselves in. She's selling you neither employment nor business ownership. She's giving you the tools, references and a step-by-step framework to judge your own situation for yourself. Live your life on your own terms – enjoy the read!'
— **Jasper Walshe**, Founder of TRIPSTank

'As an artist for over forty years, I've always struggled to understand, develop or even access the essential and fundamental skills necessary to run and build a business. Fortunately, these are Lisa's superpowers. With her values and clarity of vision around how to simplify, grow and enjoy your business, her second book is a must-read for anyone exploring their career choices at this pivotal time in history. Consider this book a parachute for the dive of your life and be safe in the knowledge that if you do jump, her first book will be there for you when you land! I would not be where I am today, or have the confidence or belief in what I do, without the wise counsel of someone who started as my business coach and is now a dear friend.'
— **Paula Barnard-Groves**, Founder of Me Infinity

'If you have ever wondered whether working for yourself is for you, this book is a great first step. Hearing first-hand from others who have taken the plunge and learning about the pros and the cons of running a business will be invaluable to your decision-making.'
— **Sophie Wright**, Founder of Wright CFO

'An inspirational and useful collection of advice from high-energy motivator Lisa Zevi. Read this before you take the plunge.'
— **Didrik Skantze**, Co-Founder of On Demand Solutions

'Setting up in business on your own is a daunting prospect, not least of which is the fear associated with all the unknowns, and the doubts that emerge about whether or not it is the right choice for you. Without the benefit of hindsight, the best any of us can do when confronting such momentous decisions is to reduce the uncertainty through rigorous research in relation to the questions we have, in order that we may forge a sense of reassurance that we have a better handle on what taking the entrepreneur's path actually entails. This book helps reduce that anxiety.'

— **Justin Lee**, Founder of Eudaimonic-Living

'Drawing upon her considerable experience as an operational business coach, Lisa Roberts Zevi has created a concise, yet masterful work that somehow manages to cover just about everything you need to know in relation to setting up and running your own business, while simultaneously offering practical strategies to help overcome the inevitable fear that pursuing your entrepreneurial dream will see you fall flat on your face. Fear of failure is part of human nature after all. Illustrated with compelling first-hand accounts, *The Business of Freedom* not only gets to the heart of the way in which the brain's negativity bias tends to engender a fear of trusting your own intuition, but it also offers some effective examples of how to overcome this ever-present doubt in order to help you recognise your worth and find your true purpose in life. Wherever you are on your journey to self-employment, I highly recommend this book to anyone looking to achieve self-actualisation through the path of entrepreneurship.'

— **Alexis Devereux**, Founder of
Capable Citizen Collective

Contents

For anyone who has ever wanted to break free and do things their way. May you find your path, conquer your fears and lead the life you deserve.

Dear Edward,

Wishing you strength, patience and joy for this next chapter.

Love Lisa x

Foreword

Deciding to take your valuable and hard-won skills out of someone else's business and into your own is a bit like jumping out of a plane for the first time. It holds that same sense of excitement and fear. You don't know what to expect or how you will feel, and you're utterly focused on getting to the ground in one piece.

Of course, you wouldn't jump out of a plane without safety gear, so why set out on this journey without the right tools to make the decision and get started? What Lisa Zevi has created in this book, is a guide to helping you do just that. *The Business of Freedom* is written specifically for individuals who are at a turning point in their career, people who are considering using their knowledge and skill in whatever area they specialise, as the core of their own business. Lisa has used her own experience of this process and added the varied experiences of other people who have been down the same route. The outcome is a thorough and thought-provoking guide that will take you step by step through the process of making the decision to run your own business, then how to define what that business might look like, and finally how to get started. You may decide not to make this change, for any number of reasons, but if you have worked through this book, it will be an informed and considered decision, based on what is right for you at this moment in time.

I am glad that you've picked this book up and are starting to read it and I would encourage you to carry on. Books are great – as long as you read them! That said, not all books are created equal. Many exist only as a kudos-generating exercise, while others contain a lot about the problem and precious little on the solution, vehicles to encourage you to buy further services from the author. This is not the case with *The Business of Freedom* or Lisa's first book *The REAL Entrepreneur*. Lisa packs her books with real-life examples, accessible information and practical activities – all of which move you forward and help you achieve your objectives.

Lisa has been helping leaders to run their teams and businesses more effectively for many years. She has experience of working in multinational corporations as well as starting and running several businesses. She works with individuals and teams during periods of transition – whether it's starting a business or scaling it, growing a strong team, or taking a step back from the day-to-day. Some people who are really good at what they do are unable to understand why others cannot do the same, but this is not the case with Lisa. Although she is incredibly capable, she is also able to dissect and explain what it is that needs to be done, and explain it in a way that is accessible for the reader.

I wonder where you are on your journey? Perhaps your idea is little more than an inkling, a quiet desire for change; perhaps you are already standing on the edge, looking down and wondering whether to leap; maybe you have already stepped out into the air and are already experiencing the exhilaration of flight and freedom and wondering where it will take you? Wherever you are, this book will keep you company, on track and help you to make good decisions.

Perhaps you have picked up this book because you are not happy in your current role? Maybe you are trying to escape an unhappy working environment? *Away from* motivation is very strong. I believe that we all deserve to work in an environment that helps us to thrive. Most of us know intuitively that we can only do our best work when we feel safe, valued, heard and appreciated by our colleagues and our bosses. Unfortunately, what many people endure is a toxic workplace where long working hours and a hostile culture drive people to self-medication of one kind or another or to burnout; this is often initiated by crappy bosses who value competition over collaboration, because they mistakenly believe people will do better if they are pitted against each other.

If you are seeking to escape a culture or company values that do not work for you, ask yourself whether finding a better employer might be the answer for you. Jobs are a little like relationships, we tend to overreact and look for something diametrically opposed to the last thing we had when something goes wrong. Do you need a sea-change or simply to find an organisation that shares your values? Turning your pottery hobby into a business may indeed be the right choice for you, but before you go down that route, take a moment to think. Could it be the environment in which you are working or the people you are working with that are making you unhappy, as opposed to the actual work you are doing? Can you afford to effectively start from scratch when you may already have a perfectly good set of revenue-generating skills on board?

What I love about this book is that Lisa really encourages you to think carefully at this point as opposed to suggesting change for change's sake. What she is saying is 'don't throw the baby out with the bathwater' until you have really checked it isn't exactly the thing you want but just in the wrong milieu.

When something is wrong, we usually have three choices: firstly, to do nothing and hope something changes to improve things or force change upon us; secondly, to adjust our attitude and learn to accept the situation and function within its limitations; and lastly, to get up and do something different. Which of these options is right for you?

We all have different preferences to risk, change and doing research. If you are someone who normally goes by your gut reaction, now may be a good time to behave out of character and take a methodical approach. Do some thorough research before moving forward. Everything comes at a cost. What is the cost of *not* making this change? If you are miserable and close to burnout then making a change could literally save your life. Research is now demonstrating the physical toll of poor mental health. I remember struggling with a big decision once and a friend looking at me kindly while delivering the killer words: 'Could you be any more unhappy?' Good question.

Your choice will depend upon your situation. What are your financial obligations, how much runway do you have? If you are single without children and you have a safety net of some sort, then perhaps you can afford to indulge your 'fly by the seat of your pants' approach. If you have a mortgage and dependents, then you may need to be more cautious for once. Lisa has created this book to guide you through the process, step by step. She will encourage you to shine a light into all the dark corners and seek evidence to support your decision, both in terms of the validity of a possible business and your suitability to run it.

I wonder what will be the catalyst that helps you make this decision. Life handed me an event which propelled me forward. I had come across an idea that struck a deep and vibrant chord with me. I knew intuitively that this was absolutely what I wanted to do. I didn't dislike my role but I was ready for a change. My creativity was stifled and I worked almost alone; what I needed was space to innovate and more connection. Then, just as I was dithering, I received an email inviting me to the funeral of a friend. Kim was a young, beautiful, kind, warm and talented woman and she was gone before I even knew she was sick. In that moment I was reminded how short and precious our lives are, that we more often regret what we don't do than what we do.

I think the scariest moment in any big change is the point when you are standing on the edge, looking down, ready to jump. One of my favourite songs is 'Watershed' by the Indigo Girls. In it they sing about standing at the fork in the road and agonising about a decision. If life has brought you to this point, it's probably a good idea to continue. You are here for a reason. Once you take that first step it gets easier – you are in it, the journey has begun and all you can do is get going.

Do I regret setting off on my own? No, not for one moment. It's been an exhilarating and rewarding journey. I've met some wonderful people, found my purpose and followed my own path. I'm able regularly to let my creativity run wild and then watch with pleasure as participants go through the learning journey I created.

I was lucky enough once to jump out of an actual plane with Lisa and it was amazing. She has written this book so that you can navigate this exciting moment in your life with her by your side. I hope you make your decision carefully and enjoy your journey.

Good luck.

Isobel Colson
The Get Going Coach, www.getgoingcoaching.co.uk

Preface

'True belonging doesn't require us to change who we are. It requires us to be who we are.'
— Brené Brown, American professor[1]

Once there was a woman who worked as a tax adviser. Let's call her Olivia. She had studied hard at school, gained a good degree at a top university and landed a well-paid job at a prestigious company. Her path was set and her parents were very proud.

The company demanded a lot from its employees, but Olivia didn't mind hard work. She worked alongside more senior members of the team, learning every day, and soon gained a reputation for being reliable and

---

1   B Brown, *Braving the Wilderness* (Random House, 2017)

thorough. She didn't have much free time, but her friends were all in high-pressured jobs too, so they grabbed time together when they could.

As her career progressed, Olivia was assigned her own clients. She seemed to have less and less time, often working into the early hours of the morning. She felt exhausted most days but told herself it would all be worth it. She loved the work. Solving problems for her clients and advising them on how to proceed gave her a great sense of satisfaction. Her clients came to rely on her expertise and recommendations, and they often referred new clients to her. The company rewarded her with promotions and bonuses.

Olivia didn't always agree with decisions made by the directors of the firm but did her best to serve her clients in line with company policies. Sometimes her manager would instruct Olivia on how to proceed. He didn't know the ins and outs of her work and sometimes suggested an approach that Olivia did not agree with. She would argue her case with him but he often wasn't interested in her perspective. She always ended up falling in line, but it didn't sit well with her.

She tried to talk to her friends. They were all so impressed with how much money she was earning, and how quickly she'd been promoted, that she found it hard to tell them about the feeling in the pit of her stomach that seemed to be growing as each week went by.

As she climbed the corporate ladder, Olivia found herself taking on larger and more prestigious clients. One day a senior partner invited her out for lunch at an expensive restaurant. She was flattered that he was taking a special interest in her and she happily answered all his questions. He pressed her about the strategy she was advising for one particular client, and she became animated as she talked about the solution she had come up with. He explained that her solution would not be the most profitable for their company. Olivia protested and insisted that it was the best option for the client.

He sat back in his chair and stared at her silently. 'There's really no need to get so emotional,' he said coldly. 'We're running a business here. Your way is not the right way.'

Olivia was mortified. She felt tears pricking at the back of her eyes. She wanted to argue but she was afraid she would end up crying, so she just nodded.

Later that day, Olivia tried to access the client's file but found it had moved. She tracked it down and found it had been assigned to a more junior colleague. Her head was spinning but she told herself to suck it up. She knew she was only a few years away from making partner, something she'd had her sights set on since she joined the firm.

The next few months were hard for Olivia. She tried to keep her head down and enjoy the work but felt like her manager was interfering much more than before. His constant criticism had her second-guessing her decisions and she felt her confidence draining away. One day the client who had been taken away called her out of the blue.

'I thought you'd like to know that I've decided to find another tax adviser,' he told her. 'The level of service has definitely deteriorated since you were reassigned.'

Olivia didn't know what to say. She didn't want to say anything negative about her employer, but she felt devastated.

After a long pause, he spoke again. 'I think you're brilliant, Olivia. You've given me such good advice over the years. I trust your judgement. If you ever decide...' he trailed off. 'Just give me a call,' he said, and hung up the phone.

That night, Olivia struggled to sleep. His words kept going round and round in her head. *What did he mean by 'if you ever decide'?* She'd had her whole career mapped out, climbing the ranks and making partner, but now she wasn't sure what she wanted. She'd never even considered a different path. She felt like she was questioning her very existence. *What is my way?*

She woke the next morning feeling strangely calm. She went into work as usual, feeling as if she was operating on autopilot. On the surface nothing had changed, but inside Olivia felt like a different person, an outsider. The corporate machine, so long a source of comfort and stability, now felt alien to her. She found herself looking at how the business was operating, trying to understand how it worked and why certain decisions were being made. She felt confused. Why was she suddenly interested in how other parts of the business operated, what other colleagues were doing? It all felt so strange, as if she was seeing her situation for the first time and questioning everything.

That afternoon, Olivia found herself in a meeting with her manager and the partner who'd taken her to lunch. They were discussing what strategy to adopt for a new and prestigious client. Suddenly the partner turned to her. 'What would you do?' he asked with a smirk. 'What's the Olivia way?'

All eyes were on her and the room fell silent. And then it hit her. She didn't belong anymore. She needed to make her own way. Without saying a word, Olivia stood up and left the room. She ran to her desk and called the client who'd left.

'I was wondering when you'd call,' he told her. 'I was just telling a supplier of mine that you'd be the person to talk to when you finally decide to…'

This time, she understood. She took a deep breath and said, 'I'd like to discuss something with you. Can I buy you lunch?'

Introduction

'Freedom is the will to be responsible to ourselves.'
— Friedrich Nietzsche, German philosopher[2]

This book is written for Olivia and people like her – people who love what they do but not all the baggage that can come from working for a large corporate. People who are fed up with the politics, interference and drama that accompany many prestigious jobs. People who want the freedom to do things their way.

This book is for you if you have a specialist set of skills that you use to provide services to clients. You could be a lawyer or an architect. Perhaps you advise clients on how to manage their finances or design their processes. Maybe you're an expert in health and safety, or

---

2   F Nietzsche, *Twilight of the Idols* (Penguin Classics, 1990). Originally published in 1889.

tax, or culture, or quality. Whatever your particular skill or area of focus, this book is for you if you love what you do but not your current situation.

People are increasingly finding the demands of corporate life less acceptable. The culture of toxic productivity has only increased during the pandemic, including the expectation that we're always available and more efficient than ever. Maybe you have a manager who keeps interfering, taking all the credit or cutting you out of situations where you should be included. Perhaps you feel constrained by the way your employer does business or the direction you're receiving. You may want to specialise or avoid that feeling of being stuck. Or it could be that you simply want to do things your way. Maybe you'd prefer to manage your own time and run things in the way *you* think they should be run.

This book is not for you if you hate what you do and want a complete change. But please don't leave until you've read about ikigai in the next chapter. It will help you get some clarity on what you might love, what path might connect you with your purpose in life and give you a sense of direction. If you're interested in running your own business, something completely different from what you do now, then my first book, *The REAL Entrepreneur: How to simplify, grow and enjoy your business*,[3] will give you a lot of useful information and things to think about.

---

3   L Zevi, *The REAL Entrepreneur: How to simplify, grow and enjoy your business* (Rethink Press, 2019)

You may be clear about what's not working for you, but not what to do about it. You could look for another job and that might carry you for a year or so, or you could seek out an alternative role in your current organisation. I suspect the reason this book has found you is that you already have a sense of what you want, you're just not sure how to go about it or how to make the decision.

Do you want more freedom? Freedom to manage your time and freedom to work with the clients you want in *your* way? Freedom to build a life that works for *you*? If so, you're probably wondering if running your own business is right for you and whether you can make it work.

There are many reasons why you may be reading this book. Perhaps you're curious about your options, maybe you're seriously considering making a change or it could even be a completely random reading choice. Whatever your reason, I'm glad you're here. Life is all about choices and you have an important one to make. Leaving paid employment is a choice I made many years ago and one I've never regretted. While the decision can seem complex, it can be made easier, and that's why I've written this book.

I can remember the exact moment I decided to leave permanent employment. I was working for a company that I, like many, considered to be one of the greatest in the world. We were presenting our region's results to our boss and his boss, the head of the division. I was in charge of rolling out a new approach to process improvement across the region and I was proud of what we'd achieved in a few short months. At the end of my presentation, the big boss complimented me on my energy and enthusiasm and delivered what he probably thought was a humorous throwaway line: 'Well done, Lisa. You really seem to believe all this s**t!'

Luckily, he didn't seem to expect a response from me. He got what he wanted from the chuckles around the table. I headed straight outside, my face burning and my head spinning. I felt like I'd been punched in the face.

I'd worked hard for the company and passionately believed in its mission. Ironically, what I was presenting that day was part of the strategy promoted by the CEO and board of the company. I was devastated to learn that he wasn't a believer.

Something died in me that day. I felt betrayed and defeated. I just didn't believe anymore. For the first time in eleven years I started working on my CV.

I formed my coaching business in 2017 and since then have worked with many entrepreneurs and business owners of all shapes and sizes across different sectors and industries. I've carved out a niche for myself as an operational business coach and my company is thriving. Delivering a TEDx talk and publishing two books are the highlights of my journey so far. I work with a small team and manage my business from wherever I am in the world, something that is critically important for me.

Over the years, I've built up a strong network who regularly refer people to me, usually business owners in need of the kind of support I provide. But every now and then, someone who's still employed will get in touch – a person from my old life who I used to work with or someone with a different set of questions: 'What's it like to work for yourself? How did you make the transition? Where do I start and what do I do?'

I want to give you the confidence and clarity to decide whether starting your own business is right for you. I want to share with you my experience of making this same transition, in the hope you can avoid some of the many mistakes I made along the way. I want to share the stories and insights of the inspiring people I met on my journey. Their honesty and courage gave me confidence, and I'm sure you'll find their contributions equally uplifting. We have each made the transition from employee to self-employed and, if you decide that's the path you want to take, then you can too.

This book is designed to be practical. I know you're a busy professional and what you need is some simple, straightforward answers.

In Part One, we'll explore some of the reasons why you might choose to stay or leave employment and set up on your own.

In Part Two, we'll walk, step by step, through the key factors in your decision. I'll introduce you to the FREEDOM Formula, which looks at all the elements you'll want to consider, including what research to do, what information is required, who you'll need to speak to, what factors need weighing and ultimately how to make the decision.

In Part Three, we'll look at some of the different options you can choose from, plus the practicalities of starting and running a business. We'll also discuss how to stay the course and ensure that your business works for you.

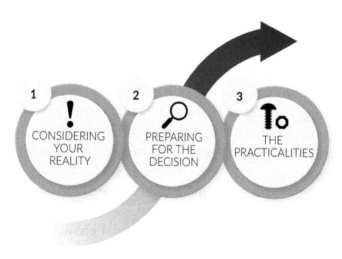

Interviews

Many have trodden the path you're considering taking. I was fortunate to be able to interview people at various stages of the process. Some were still in employment while others had recently left. Several had been running businesses for years and some were considering a return to employment. Many are named in this book while others chose to remain anonymous. I would like to thank each and every one of them for sharing their wisdom. I'm sure that, like me, you'll find their insights inspiring.

Andy Pieroux: Andy is the managing director of Walpole Partnership, a boutique consultancy firm specialising in Configure, Price, Quote (CPQ). He established the company in 2013 and has built up a team of specialists who deliver projects to a wide range of clients.

Anish Hindocha: Anish set up Jigsaw Change Consulting in 2019 to help teams in financial services develop better workplace cultures by improving things like their meetings and their decision-making. He describes it as 'workplace transformation at a team level.'

Austin Peat: Austin is one of two founders of a UK-based research consultancy that started in 2010. It began by focusing on Russia and the former Soviet Union and has since expanded its geographical scope to Europe and North America. They provide services in three main areas – strategic research, due diligence and corporate communication – to clients including multilateral institutions, financial organisations, law firms, companies, investors and advisers.

Caroline Somer: Caroline runs Somer Design, a full-scale brand and digital marketing agency based in London. She manages a core team of creatives, from content writers and graphic designers to web developers and digital marketing experts, pooling talent from across the world.

Didrik Skantze: Didrik worked as a technical consultant for a large company before deciding to join a small group of specialists to form On Demand Solutions.

Francis West: Francis is originally from South Africa and came to the UK as a young man. He's always been entrepreneurial and looking for opportunities – 'By the age of ten, I was already pushing trolleys.' He told me he hates being told what to do and the only way he can 'fix the problems' is by running his own business. He started Westtek, an IT services company, in 2010.

Justin Lee: Justin is a former recruiter who, after six years of training and clinical practice, is now a fully qualified psychotherapist. Although his two careers appear on the face of it to be very different, people are at the heart of both. He told me that his focus has always been on integrity and helping people 'self-actualise'.

Katy Hampton: Katy is a minimum wage and fair pay specialist. She works with companies who are being investigated by HMRC. Our interview took place on her first day of working for herself, having left a top accountancy firm the day before.

Nancy Lamb: Nancy is a qualified solicitor and construction contract specialist who started her own business in April 2021. She specialises in reading construction contracts and helping people avoid disputes.

Sophie Wright: Sophie is a part-time Chief Financial Officer (CFO) who set up Wright CFO in 2014. She works with several clients directly but also recruits other CFOs and places them with clients.

Tamara Makoni: Tamara is a culture consultant who at the time of our interview was on the verge of resigning from her job and starting her own business. She specialises in intercultural understanding and communication.

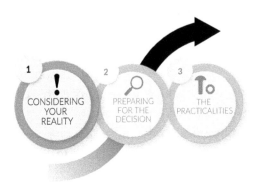

PART ONE

CONSIDERING YOUR REALITY

The opportunities provided by many large companies can be exciting and rewarding, and for many years I couldn't imagine a different life. I grew up in the corporate world. It was where I built my foundations, honed my skills and learned how to work with others. Working in a large company can also be tough. Many people don't realise the toll it's taking on them until after they leave or suffer a mental health crisis.

It can be hard to let go of the prestige that working for a large company gives you. Working for Xerox was part of my identity. I still can't walk past a photocopier without checking out which brand it is! When you're employed, you're paid to do a specific job which serves a purpose laid out by someone else. That's part of the deal. In small companies, you may have the opportunity to influence the direction of the business as well as its culture and values, but in larger companies, that's more of a challenge. You can end feel up feeling like a small cog in a big, powerful, heartless machine.

Don't get me wrong, I'm incredibly grateful for the years I spent in the corporate world, for everything I learned and the experience I gained. But there comes a time for many people when it's no longer worth the price you pay.

The pandemic has had an impact on us all. For some there are huge opportunities, while others face devastating losses. It's forced or perhaps encouraged many of us to look at our lives and ask ourselves what we really want. The way we work has changed. Business owners and managers have had to learn how to manage and motivate remote teams and build flexible working practices into their business models. We've had to adapt to video calls, background noise and our home life interfering or blending with our work life in ways that we couldn't have conceived previously. More than ever before, questions about where we want to live, what kind of work–life balance we want and how we'd like to be spending our time have been able to come to the fore.

It may seem like a crazy time to be considering leaving a well-paid job and taking the risk of starting out on your own. But the truth is that if your current situation isn't working for you, you owe it to yourself to look at the alternatives.

CHAPTER 1

What Do You Want?

> 'One half of knowing what you want is knowing
> what you must give up before you get it.'
> — Sydney Howard, American playwright[4]

I've always encouraged my clients to start with what they *want* rather than what they *think* is possible. But knowing what we want has to start with being honest with ourselves.

As modern human beings, we can feel compelled to create the perfect impression of ourselves even when things don't feel right. In some cases, this may be due to over- or under-confidence, while in others it may actually be self-deception. If you're struggling to stay positive and focused, it could be that you're not being entirely honest with yourself. When we're deceiving

---

4   From *They Knew What They Wanted*, a play by Sydney Howard, 1924

ourselves, we choose to see what we want while ignoring what we'd prefer not to have to deal with. This may provide short-term happiness or relief, but in the long run, it's unhealthy and destructive.

There may be good reasons for you wanting to protect yourself from facing the reality of your situation, but when we lie to ourselves, more and more of our energy gets used to keep up the deception, which is exhausting and can stop us feeling energised and wanting to move forward. Getting clear about what you really want, even if it scares you, will feel better than keeping up any deception you may have been living with.

I had a coaching session with a new client who wanted to become more disciplined. He was able to clearly articulate why it was important to him to have a morning routine. He described the activities he'd like to include and the benefits of each – a nourishing breakfast, some reading or learning to feed his brain, and exercise to move his body.

We talked about the reality: spontaneous evenings, late nights watching videos in bed and lack of willpower in the mornings. 'I'm just coasting from one day to the next,' he told me. 'All those benefits, the reasons why I should be doing all that, just don't seem very important when the alarm goes off!'

I asked him what the benefits of coasting were to him and then let the silence fill the space. When he started talking, it was more to himself than to me. He realised that he hadn't been honest with himself. He was actually allowing himself time to process the fallout of a painful personal event in the previous year, without really admitting it. He understood in that moment that he was making a choice to coast and that when he was ready to change things, he would be able to do so. Instead of using the big stick and so many 'shoulds', he was able to see that he needed some time and that he could choose to be kind to himself. It suddenly became clear to him that he hadn't yet made the decision to become more disciplined. This came as a huge relief.

Honesty with ourselves not only has a positive impact on our own lives but also on the people around us. Being authentic allows us to stay positive even when life is tough. It enables us to look for solutions rather than running away or sticking our head in the sand. It also allows us to acknowledge the self-deception we sometimes use to mask our problems and shield ourselves from pain. Until we accept who we are, in entirety, we cannot begin to move forward or build the life we want.

Maybe you know people who have taken flowers to a colleague in hospital whom they despise, sang the praises of their annoying boss, married just because society expects it, or stayed in relationships that have been dead for years. The dishonesty of such situations has a profoundly negative impact on people's lives. They end up despising their partner, resenting their boss, and even losing their sense of identity.

Living an honest life means accepting reality. It can mean making tough decisions such as filing for divorce to regain your self-confidence, choosing to let go of a promising career that's draining you physically and emotionally, or cutting ties with people who are dragging you off track. Being honest with yourself can be painful but highly rewarding. When you combine honesty with your willingness to change, there's no limit to the ways you can grow and improve.

One of the things I've learned over the years is that many of us don't acknowledge what we're truly capable of. We underestimate ourselves and others and we allow ourselves to focus on all the reasons why something won't or can't happen.

I see it often in my coaching work – clients who dismiss what they want as selfish or unachievable, telling themselves they are being unrealistic or arrogant. When left unchallenged, this way of thinking is incredibly limiting. It means you never allow yourself to become clear about what you actually want. Your dreams remain nebulous and so difficult to achieve. As they never become reality, you reinforce your belief that they were never possible anyway. It's a terribly damaging cycle that diminishes your potential by encouraging you to think small rather than dreaming big.

What would happen if you indulged yourself instead? Allow yourself to get really clear about that wild and crazy ambition of yours. Write down your ideal scenario without limits or compromise – in detail.

The truth is that dreams don't exist only when we're sleeping. Almost anything is possible with hard work, determination and clear goals.

We all spend so much time trying to figure out *how* to do things, when actually the most difficult question is figuring out *what* we want. The miraculous thing is that when you get clear on *what* you want, the *how* starts falling into place. Our brains are so much more powerful than we realise and most of their work is done below the surface.

Let me give you an example. A few years ago, I received a call from my mother, who, like me, is a restless soul.

'I miss my home, Lisa,' she told me. 'I just need a bit of stability in my life.'

She'd wanted a job that meant she could travel, deal with different people and be performing a variety of activities. She applied for roles that met her criteria and happily worked for several years as a companion for a few different elderly people on a rotating basis. Now she was calling me to tell me it wasn't working for her.

'Are your requirements of a job still the same?' I asked her. 'Maybe you need to revisit them.'

My mother realised that what she wanted had changed over time. We talked about what would work for her now. She decided that she needed something more settled, where she could explore more of her interests. A few days later, she heard about a job at the local college. They were looking for someone to oversee the preparation of lunches for their students. My mother is an excellent cook and loves managing a team. 'It sounds like my perfect job,' she told me, and so it turned out to be!

Often, we don't actually stop and ask ourselves what we want. We proceed along a path we've chosen without checking back that it's still right for us. Getting really clear about what we want and what will give our working lives meaning is not always easy. Some are lucky enough to have found that *thing* that gets them out of bed feeling energised and alive. That incredible sense of fulfilment knowing that what they do is making a difference. Others are still searching for their purpose, their passion, their flow.

Your drivers

In my coaching work, I meet people at many different stages of life. Some are connected to their purpose, while others struggle with decision-making and motivation. It can be a challenge to get clear about what really drives you. The experiences and choices you've made along the way have brought you to this point and shape the way you view the world. Perhaps you watched your mother struggle with money growing up, as I did. Maybe you crave stability or adventure, visible success or inner tranquillity. You may be driven by a desire to leave a legacy for those who come after you.

If you feel driven to serve, it may come from a desire to protect others from negative experiences you've had. One of my first clients lost her mother as a teenager and set up a charity to help children deal with trauma. 'I wish I'd had that kind of support when I was growing up,' she told me.

One of my interviewees, Francis, aims to educate and protect over one million people from cyberattacks, having lost his previous business to unscrupulous fraudsters. 'The more I learn, the more I want to protect,' he said. He had to start a new business from scratch in 2010. 'I had a family to provide for,' he told me. 'I had to make it work.'

Here's a tool I use to help clients get clear about their options and their motivation.

Tool – Ikigai

There's an ancient Japanese concept called ikigai, which literally means 'worth living for' or your 'reason for being'.[5] It's a powerful way of looking at our lives and our work. For many, their ikigai is their family. Having ikigai in your work is not so common, but I believe that it's a vital goal to aim for.

The ikigai model is often depicted as four interlocking circles.

The first circle shows what you're good at – what strengths, skills and experience do you have? Next, what you love – what really drives and motivates you? At the intersection of these two circles is your **passion**.

The third circle shows what the world needs – what do you feel compelled to change in the world? At the intersection of what you love and what the world needs is your **mission**.

The fourth circle shows what you can get paid for – what is worth money? At the intersection of what you can get paid for and what the world needs is your **vocation**, and at the intersection of what you can get paid for and what you're good at is your **profession**.

In the centre of these four interlocking circles is your **ikigai**.

---

5   H Garcia and F Mirales, *Ikigai: The Japanese secret to a long and happy life* (Penguin Life, 2017)

It's easy to get tempted by all the things we could do, and it's a huge privilege to live in an age where so much is possible, but ikigai helps us focus on what we feel drawn to do.

Everybody deserves to love what they do and do what they love. This book is written for people who love what they do but want to do it their way. Later in this book, we'll look at some pros and cons of leaving employment and working for yourself. Bear this in mind as you read through the next pages.

Be warned though. There's also something one of my interviewees, Anish, has termed the 'ikigai trap', which we discussed during our interview. He left a corporate job to set up his own consultancy practice focusing on workplace culture. 'People over-index on what they love and what they're good at,' he told me. 'They convince themselves that the world needs it, and that people will therefore pay for it.' It's critically important that you pay equal attention to all four aspects of ikigai.

The catalyst

What are your reasons for picking up this book? Maybe the decision of whether to stay in paid employment is one you've been mulling for some time. Perhaps there's a nagging doubt in your mind that something isn't quite right. Or it could be that, like me, you've had a sudden realisation that things need to change.

Many people find their relationship with the organisation and the people they work with evolving over time. One of my interviewees compared starting a new job with the beginning of a new relationship. They talked about ignoring all the things they didn't like and focusing on those they did. But as they became more senior in their organisation, they found their role more difficult. 'I felt very restricted,' they told me. 'My rose-tinted spectacles didn't work anymore.' They described feeling suffocated and finding the lack of freedom challenging. Their catalyst was a particular meeting during which they felt they'd been betrayed by their colleagues. 'I realised I wasn't really in a team. There wasn't any loyalty. It was a massive kick in the gut.'

Often the feeling of wanting to do your own thing builds over many months, even years. Anish told me he'd set up a web domain and company three years before he left his large corporate employer. 'I couldn't go then. We'd found out we were expecting our second child and we needed some stability and security. But I had this itch that I wanted to scratch.' When the opportunity presented itself years later, he was ready to start his own consultancy firm.

Sophie decided to take redundancy from her job after the birth of her second child and took on a short-term contract. She found herself working long hours including a lengthy commute to and from work. 'I was basically being a bad everything,' she told me. 'A bad parent, a bad worker!' She made a series of choices, the first of which was to stop commuting, which led to her having conversations with smaller companies closer to where she lived. The decision to set up her own business providing outsourced CFO services quickly followed.

For you, it may be a sense that things need to change or a set of circumstances that points you in a particular direction. Often when things change unexpectedly, new possibilities become apparent. Austin told me it was a combination of circumstance, location and network that led him to set up his consultancy business. He described that the 'pressure, remuneration and culture' of working in investment banking created 'a pervasive internal dialogue of *Should I stay or should I go?*'. His job came to a natural end just before the global financial crisis hit and he decided to strike out with a new business partner. He told me he's 'never looked back, despite working at least as hard as in investment banking.'

Caroline was another casualty of the financial crisis. She'd always wanted to run her own business, but it hadn't felt right when her children were small. When her corporate employer offered her redundancy, she knew it was the right time. 'It was a reasonable settlement which gave me the financial security to start my own brand and marketing business.'

Your catalyst may be about finding the right balance between your work and personal life. Juggling the expectations of work and home can leave little time for looking after yourself. Nancy found herself working through an entire holiday, managing several projects in the construction industry. 'I was incredibly stressed,' she told me. 'My son and my husband were very forgiving when they shouldn't have been.' She then suffered the trauma of a miscarriage. 'I'm not saying the two are connected,' she said, 'but those two things combined just made me stop and go, "*This is ridiculous. This is not what I want to be doing or how I want to be living.*"' She told me about the moment she realised that she wanted to 'stop surviving and start living.'

One of the motivating factors for many is the sense that your own values are diverging from your employer's. You may have a sense that you don't 'fit' as well as you once did, or the number of compromises you feel you're having to make is increasing. For Tamara, it was 'a growing feeling that a conventional career path couldn't offer what I wanted and was actively holding me back.' She described being unhappy in her communications job and knowing that she wanted to do something different.

Didrik took a more unusual route. The project he had been working on was winding down and he was no longer feeling motivated or inspired by his job. 'I felt like a tourist staying in a resort when most of the other guests had left,' he told me, 'and the autumn weather was starting to roll in!' He was looking for a small company to invest some savings in and ended up joining as a co-founder.

A critical reason for one of my interviewees to make the change was their own personal sense of purpose: 'that's what ultimately gave me the direction to sail off in', they said. For many years they'd felt a 'huge sense of urgency and responsibility for the future of our planet and all the species that live on it.' They described the disconnect they felt between the public-facing brand of their Big Four employer, which scores highly on measures of sustainability (something they says reflects the immaturity of sustainability reporting and the strength of the PR machine), and the reality they experienced on the ground as an employee. 'They don't give a damn about anything other than their own profit.' They told me they just couldn't stay in an environment where they weren't spending their days focused on their purpose.

For some, the decision to leave paid employment is triggered by a single defining moment. Often the feelings of unease or discomfort have been around for some time, but it can take a particular action or event to change how the individual sees the world and their place in it. For me, it was like a slap in the face. I felt like I was suddenly seeing things in a new way, things that had always been there but that I'd been ignoring.

One of my interviewees talked about having day-dreamed about flexibility and freedom for a long time but the pivotal event for them was when their employer refused to honour a financial agreement. 'It made me question everything,' they told me. 'I felt they didn't value me. It was a breakdown of trust. I was just a number.' They made a plan and handed in their notice.

Justin described it as a 'penny-dropping light bulb' moment. Although he'd felt disenfranchised for some time, his catalyst emerged when a loved one got cancer for the second time. He decided to read up about her condition and discovered psycho-neuro-immunology, which highlighted the importance of addressing not just the physiological components of the disease but also the psychological. Having always been interested in psychology and reading up on diverse and seemingly unrelated topics like epigenetics and systems thinking, suddenly everything came together and his calling became clear. 'Fascination is the birthplace of creativity,' he told me. In his case, it was a new professional career as a psychotherapist.

People have various reasons to leave paid employment and there are many different routes to business ownership. Some consider leaving but ultimately find a job that suits them. Others try out working for themselves only to conclude that it's not for them.

I'm always fascinated to hear people's stories and the reasons why they chose the path they did. Whatever your story, I've written this book to help you decide what's right for you. Let's look at some of the reasons why you might choose to leave your job or stay in employment.

CHAPTER 2

Reasons To Go

'Change the way you look at things, and the things you look at change.'
— Wayne W Dyer, American self-help and spiritual author[6]

You may be feeling uncertain. It's a big decision and some people you talk to may not understand why it's even a question in your head. You have a good job, you're well paid, you're successful. So why are you even considering putting all that at risk?

You may simply feel the need for a change, like Austin, who took the opportunity the financial crisis offered him. He told me about wanting to do something different 'while age and circumstances allowed.'

---

6 W Dyer, 'Success secrets', www.drwaynedyer.com/blog/success-secrets

For me, it was a matter of freedom. I loved what I was doing but it was consuming me, plus I felt like I was getting too *narrow*. Same office every day, same people, same challenges. I wanted more freedom to plan my time, to take on multiple clients, to choose who I worked with. I also wanted to be able to effect change at an organisational level.

You want to do things your way

Whatever autonomy you have in your current role, someone else is still ultimately calling the shots. There may come – or have come – a time when you simply want to have control over your own time and how you do the work you do. During the pandemic, boundaries between the different parts of our lives have become blurred and that's meant many people choosing to reprioritise aspects of their lives.

Psychotherapist Justin describes himself as someone who's constantly analysing and being creative. 'But if I'm putting forward ideas, and nine times out of ten they're falling on deaf ears, then what's the point?' He realised that he thrives when he's able to be creative and do his own thing without constraints. Anish also spoke about creativity. 'Corporates put guard-rails or parameters around what your job is. All that melts away when you leave. I've changed what I do from process improvement consultant to a culture transformation expert. And that change was not going to happen if I was working for a corporate.'

Many people have a clear sense of how they feel things *should* be done. If that's you then you may find it draining working with people who don't feel the same. Sophie told me that even as a junior financial analyst, she always had an opinion about how the business she worked in should be run. 'Now I'm able to do it how I think it should be done.'

Freedom is a big motivator for many people considering this transition. 'When you start,' Nancy told me, 'it's just about doing it for yourself, it's about standing on your own two feet, it's about not being controlled by somebody else. It's about saying, "I know what I'm doing, you lot are just making it more difficult than it needs to be!"' Katy was looking for more freedom and more control over her own decisions. 'The flexibility to be able to choose when and where I work from, working with whoever I want and also being in control of my finances.' Anish described it as looking at pistachio ice cream and being told that you could only have vanilla. 'You just see this palette of stuff that you can do, and I wanted to pivot and get uncomfortable.'

You feel unappreciated

For some, it comes down to not feeling appreciated in their current position. Maybe you have a boss who micromanages or takes all the credit for your hard work. If you're the one who has the relationship with the client, does the work and has the skills, it's not too much of a leap to consider taking the next logical step and setting up on your own. Large companies are often inefficient, something that really bothered one of my interviewees. 'The amount of time it took to make a decision plus watching my manager searching online for the best deals on rugby tickets while criticising us for not doing a better job, started to really wear me down.' They told me they didn't hesitate when they were offered redundancy. 'I realised it was my time.'

You can't find what you're looking for in other paid roles

Starting your own business may not be the first place your mind goes when you realise your job isn't working for you anymore. Tamara's first instinct when she realised she was unhappy in her job was to look for a new one. After spending many months trying to find the right role, she concluded that none of the roles she was going for were really hitting the mark. It was her partner who suggested that she set up her own business and although she initially found the idea 'really scary', more and more, she said, 'I felt it was my only option if I wanted to progress and build something for me.' She described how over time the idea built and started to really excite her. 'I'm looking forward to throwing myself into it and really making it my own.'

If you've got that drive to do things your own way, you've probably got lots of ideas about how you'll do things differently. In Chapter 10 (Offer), we'll look at ways to package your services.

You want to do more

Large companies aren't usually structured to leverage people's natural talents. Many invest significant sums on training their employees to improve on their weaknesses, rather than encouraging them to play to their strengths. 'My entire potential wasn't being tapped,' Anish told me. 'I thought, *I could do so much more than this. You're letting me use 10% of what I can do*, and that was frustrating.' He described making an 'outsized impact' with the other 90% he was giving, but without permission or being aligned to the company's objectives.

You may find you're feeling a bit stale and in need of a new challenge. Andy had been working for a large corporate for many years and was feeling his career had 'plateaued'. He first made an internal move to a new role within the organisation, which solved the problem for a while, but he felt 'the march of time. A feeling that if it was going to happen, I needed to get on with it.'

Nancy talked about wanting to specialise. 'I'd always felt a bit lost. I've never really fitted anywhere.' She told me how all the different things she'd done in her life now made sense and were coming together and helping her define what she wanted moving forward. We talked about the feeling of finding your own lane and really sticking to it.

You want to earn more

If you're being charged out to your employer's clients, your salary may not reflect the effort you think you're putting in or what you believe you're worth. 'I felt very strongly that I would be able to earn more money and have more time than I could on a permanent salary,' Anish said.

Maybe you've been promised a greater slice of the pie, but it hasn't materialised. One of my clients felt betrayed by her employer. She'd been promised a promotion and a big bonus that never came. She felt her boss was constantly making her beg for attention and trying to cut her out of deals. She knew that things needed to change and approached me to work through her need for approval and her fear of being self-sufficient. We worked on putting in boundaries with her current boss before she took the plunge to venture out on her own.

If you're not in a client-facing role but instead focused on serving internal stakeholders as I was, it can be trickier to figure out what you're worth in monetary terms. You may still believe you could earn more doing your own thing. Nancy told me she decided to find a way to take control of her life and use her skills and experience 'not to line someone else's pockets.' Katy talked about 'time and financial flexibility.'

Fear of missing out, of failing to reach your potential, of being left behind, may also be reasons why you're considering this change. Anish told me that when he was offered redundancy, he immediately saw the opportunity to start his own business. But one of his team was terrified about how he was going to get another role. He was a few years older than Anish, who said to himself, 'I cannot let that happen to me. I cannot rely on a single company to pay my bills. I can do more. I want to be master of my own destiny. Let's do this.'

Earning what you're worth and achieving more may be motivating you to consider a change. In Chapter 6 (Research), we'll look at how to assess the market and figure out your potential.

The corporate world is no longer serving you

Burnout is a common problem in the corporate world. You may be working too many hours or trying too hard to please. Maybe you don't have proper boundaries in place with your work or your boss. Perhaps you're considering doing your own thing as a way of working fewer hours or more flexibly.

You may not be conscious of the impact your working life is having on you. Sophie, who now provides outsourced CFO services to small businesses, shared with me the moment she realised just how much of a drain the politics of big-company life had on her. 'Rarely did I get a chance to just do the work. All the other stuff took up so much of my brain. It was quite a big revelation when I realised that. I had no idea.'

In many large companies, the people at the top make a lot of money from the 'cannon fodder'. Fresh young things that are snapped up straight from university and indoctrinated into the corporate culture of working in a certain way and conforming, regardless of the cost to their mental and physical health. Nancy talked about being sucked into the corporate machine and being told it was the only way forward. Everyone is expected to dress the same and behave the same and 'authenticity is oppressed.' She told me a story of not having a suit jacket with her one day and her colleagues being scandalised. She wasn't even meeting clients, but not wearing the 'uniform' was still frowned upon. 'It was stifling,' she told me.

There's a lot of status and cachet associated with working for a household name that can be hard to give up. Nancy described a 'eureka moment' when she let go of the 'emotional attachment' to her previous life as a corporate lawyer. She told me that, in her experience, people who make this transition have had 'a niggle in the back of our heads from early on. We fight it and fight it because of social conditioning and then something happens, and you think, *I'm not doing this anymore.*' Her view is that many professionals, people like lawyers and accountants, are conditioned to believe the only way to be successful is a certain path. 'When that doesn't fit and it doesn't feel right, you feel like a failure.' She described trying to fight those feelings and having to break the 'professional and social conditioning'. She believes that many professionals see business ownership and entrepreneurship as 'reckless' and told me it definitely goes against the grain.

There's a tension that exists in many companies between doing what's right for the business and what's right for the individuals who work for it. It's a subject that comes up frequently in my coaching sessions. In small companies, the needs of the individual and the needs of the business are easier to align. But in most large organisations, you're very much part of the 'machine'. One interviewee told me they reached the point where they realised, 'However senior you are, you are their asset to deploy as they see fit. They come first and you don't.' I know several people who've worked for Big Four consultancies, and their experiences were similar. Another interviewee explained it like this: 'I'm serving somebody else's idea of a business model. I realised I had two choices – either accept the model or walk away. It wasn't an option for me to stay and whinge.'

Big companies are good at instilling in you the need to be busy. The busier you are, the more valuable. I've come to understand that I tend to see my own value through being busy. When I'm busy, I feel productive and useful, but I've learned that I can add much more value when I slow down. Learning to see your own value through what you achieve rather than how busy you are is a key element in avoiding burnout.

Burnout had been a pattern of mine for years and one I was determined to leave behind when I started my coaching business.

My story: 'How many more times do you want to go round this again?'

Have you ever had an out-of-body experience?

It was December 2017, and I was up on the stage in a large auditorium. It was a live training day on my coaching training and I'd volunteered to help the trainer demonstrate the conversation where you and the client decide if they want to work together. The trainer came across as a brisk, no-nonsense type of person – somewhat fearsome but with a hint of a wicked sense of humour beneath the surface. I was wrestling with how to prioritise all the different things I wanted to be focusing on and I seized the opportunity to get some advice. But the role-play wasn't going as planned.

'I always used to get close to burnout when I was working in those big companies – the corporates and investment banks, and now I'm so busy and trying to do too much, I'm worried I might be doing it again,' I said. 'Except before, I could always just change jobs and go travelling in between, but this time I can't. This is my business. My clients. And I don't want to have to give it all up.'

'What's keeping you so busy?' she asked me.

'I'm writing a book, I'm swamped with clients, I'm building programmes...' I tailed off as she took the opportunity to do an aside to the audience.

'Lisa isn't one of those people who struggles to get clients.' (This brought about lots of groans from my fellow students.) 'You might want to chat to her about that!'

'Starting something, almost burning myself out, then leaving. I think it's a bit of a cycle...' I heard myself say the words and saw her piercing eyes fix me with a look as she asked her killer question.

'How many more times do you want to go round this again?'

Suddenly, I was looking at myself. On stage. In front of hundreds of people. Hesitating!

'How many more times?' she asked again.

One part of my brain was screaming at me to tell her, *Never again, I'm not ever getting close to burnout again.* But another part was seriously considering whether two or three more times was an option.

In that moment, I realised I had a problem. I'd been in denial about burnout. Many of us have cycles we run – mine is burnout. To be honest, it's something I'm still working through to this day.

It's not a straightforward decision to leave a dynamic workplace with high-calibre colleagues, challenging work and interesting clients. If you love what you do, it can be a tough decision to leave, even if you know you'll be able to keep many aspects of the actual work. One of my interviewees describes the fascinating work they did at their Big Four employer as, 'Great experience, great clients, amazing people. It's not without value being in that environment.' But they found themself having to balance that with 'the absolute burnout of working consistently seventy hours a week.'

Burnout is a real issue for many people and starting your own business is unlikely to fix it. I work with many people who struggle with finding the right balance for them. In Chapter 11 (Mindset), we'll look at how to avoid burnout in your own business.

CHAPTER 3

Reasons To Stay

'Acknowledging the good that you already have in your life is the foundation for all abundance.'
— Eckhart Tolle, German spiritual teacher[7]

There are many reasons why people choose to stay in employment long past the moment they first thought of leaving. There are also likely to be many opinions to consider, starting with the voice of caution in your own head.

Didrik's brain was telling him, *I am an adult; I should make wise decisions. On paper, this is not a wise decision!*

Once you tell someone how you're feeling and what you're considering, others may urge you to think twice, to weigh the risks. Austin talked about the 'many ostensible reasons for being an employee,

---

7 E Tolle, *A New Earth: Awakening to your life's purpose* (Plume, 2005)

including so-called job security, defined time off and financial visibility, much of which can be illusionary.' He talked about weighing up the benefits of working in a dynamic sector with highly intelligent people with the drawbacks, such as the inevitable pigeon-holing that comes from being in a large organisation.

The primary function of our brains is to keep us safe, and by definition, change is a step into the unknown and so fraught with risk. Our brains don't like risk, so if you decide to take this step, you'll have to overcome some of the objections that your own brain and well-meaning people might present you with.

Your job gives you security

The biggest fear that many people have when considering leaving their job is the loss of security and stability. That regular payment into your bank account is a comforting sight. Thinking about 'losing' your pay cheque is enough to make most people pause. It's natural to question whether you'll be able to pay the bills, maintain your lifestyle and keep a roof over your head. 'Having an assured income every month provides a lot of comfort and reassurance,' Tamara told me. 'Thinking about no longer having that, choosing to give it up, can feel like a crazy prospect.'

The truth is, there's no safety net when you work for yourself, apart from the one you create, and that can be a scary reality to face. Nancy told me she feared 'no one would take me on, that I'd have no money and I'd have to borrow money from my husband!' She acknowledged the incredibly fortunate position she was in, having a safety net which meant it was OK if she didn't earn any money for a few months.

The topic of money was raised by many of the people I interviewed. 'Don't fool yourself,' Didrik told me. 'It's a big and important decision. If you can't afford it, don't do it!'

'The biggest fear was, and always will be, loss of income,' Sophie said. She described how important it is to 'have the stomach for it', but added that, in her view, a bit of fear around money is probably sensible. 'I've got commitments,' she told me. 'I can't just move into a studio apartment if this doesn't work out!'

Fear is natural and inevitable, so it's important to think about strategies you can use to overcome yours. Think about what makes you feel calm and confident. Austin described having a fear of the unknown, which he overcame by committing to working and learning as much as possible. Like many considering this move, he was concerned about whether he could make enough to both live and save for the future. 'Practising financial discipline, particularly in the early days,' he told me, 'plus having a bit of trial period, was useful to help me overcome my fears.'

Interestingly, the fear of financial failure can really help focus your mind. 'As the sole breadwinner in our family at the time, I couldn't afford a vanity project or a hobby,' Andy said.

But there's also another side to financial concerns. 'Financial security is important,' one interviewee told me, 'but when I wasn't paid the bonus I was expecting, it made me realise I wanted to be in control of my own finances.' The thought of not being able to pay your bills can be terrifying. 'I spent far too long worrying about ending up with nothing, no money,' they told me. 'But because I think in that way, I would never let it happen. Now all I see is opportunities.'

The question I hear many people asking is, 'Where does my security actually come from?' The security of a permanent job is not what it once was, which is leading more people to consider how they feel about relying on their own efforts and plotting their own path. 'I have the self-confidence,' one interviewee told me. 'I knew if I needed to prioritise making money, I'd make money. I know I can do that.' Nevertheless, they admitted to a 'healthy amount of financial fear.'

There's a long road between your current salary and being destitute and unable to pay the bills, a road that contains decisions and opportunities. There's always the option of getting another job, even if it doesn't pay as well as your current one. Short-term pieces of work can also help pay the bills. In Chapter 7 (Earnings), we'll look at how to put a plan together and figure out your numbers.

You don't have the confidence to go it alone

It's not uncommon for us to struggle to see our own value and that might make you pause when considering leaving paid employment. Not only do we not see ourselves well, but we also forget that what comes naturally to us is unnatural or strange to others. Intellectually we know we're all different, and yet it doesn't occur to us that something we do easily can be a struggle for others, that the connections we make naturally are their blind spots. This is one of the reasons why it's important to get external perspectives.

My story: 'What's the name of that volcano over there – can I climb it?!'

I've always admired creative people who spot opportunities and build businesses and I had a very successful career working with them and helping them implement their ideas. Unlike them, I never thought of myself as an entrepreneur. They're the people with ideas and strategies that can spot gaps in the market. That's not me. My superpower is helping people get clear. I'm a right-hand woman, an implementer. The one who organises, manages and gets things done.

And yet in March 2017, I found myself in an auditorium full of entrepreneurs and business owners. The speaker had brown hair, a smart jacket, shiny shoes and a big smile. He was bathed in bright lights, and talking about being an entrepreneur. I caught the eye of my friend Andy, the owner of a boutique consultancy firm that sells specialist sales software. We've known each other for more than twenty years. He was volunteering at the event and the reason I was there – 'Just come along. It'll be fun, I promise you. I'll even pay for your ticket. You said you were looking for something different!'

'Yes, but I didn't mean something for business owners, it'll just be a waste of time,' I grumbled.

'You've helped me such a lot with my business, Lisa. This is my gift to you!'

And so there I was, feeling like an imposter. Even the name 'Brand Accelerator' seemed alien to me!

The speaker started describing a time when he was in Bali, and my ears pricked up. Travelling was something I *did* know about.

'We'd just landed,' he said. 'We're jet lagged and exhausted and I'm looking out of the car all bleary eyed and half-asleep and I see this volcano and I immediately want to climb it.'

Have you ever been in a situation where someone's speaking to lots of people, but you feel like they're talking directly to you? I *love* climbing volcanos and now I was hanging on every word.

'You wake up early one morning and you start the climb before dark. It's hard work and it hurts, and you wonder whether it'll be worth it.'

I knew exactly where he was going with this story – the view is *so* worth it. Whenever I see any kind of high-up place that might have a superb view, I want to climb it. There's something about being *up* that I just love. My husband always jokes about me that anything called 'Mirador', 'Vista point', 'Viewpoint' – I'm there! He's much stronger and fitter than me and he walks fast. I've got used to the fact that he's usually one or two steps ahead. It's frustrating, but walking fast takes the fun away for me.

Imagine my delight when we visited Guatemala in 2013 – my very first time at any serious altitude – and decided to climb a volcano. I felt strong and I was striding forth, while he struggled behind me. I'm not competitive (much), but it did feel great to be ahead for once. In the years that have followed, we've climbed several volcanos and it's always been the same – he struggles, and I'm like a mountain goat. Apparently older women do much better at altitude than very fit, stocky men like my wonderful husband. If it's the only time I get to feel stronger than him, I'll take it!

The speaker was describing the view as he neared to the summit. I could picture it in my mind. The lush green fields, the mist and the exquisite sunset. I was there with him in beautiful Bali at the top of that volcano. Suddenly he asked, 'What's the name of *that* volcano over there – can I climb that one?' and I burst out laughing, because that's exactly what I said when we got to the top in Guatemala! There was another beautiful volcano that we could see from where we were standing. I asked about climbing it and the guide replied, 'What about the one you're standing on?'

The speaker's point was exactly that, and it was a life-changing moment for me. As I listened to him talk about the 'Mountain of Value' that each and every one of us is standing on, I began to see that everything I'd learned both in the corporate world and in investment banking – how to manage people, how to build teams and how to organise anything and everything – could be used to help entrepreneurs and business owners.

It took me a while to recognise my own value and I want to help you see yours. You have a set of skills and experiences that may be valuable to others, even if they come naturally to you. Your perspective and particular way of approaching a problem and finding solutions is unique, and that's what you're considering taking out to the market. It can be intimidating and scary to start with, but I promise it gets easier with time. It all starts with talking to people and telling them what you do.

After the speaker had finished telling us about our 'Mountain of Value', he did what I'd been absolutely dreading and asked us to introduce ourselves to three people around us. I took a deep breath and said, 'Hello, my name is Lisa and I'm an implementer. I help people simplify, grow and enjoy their businesses.' It sounded weird to me, but it also felt good. I'd defined myself for so long as a person who worked for someone else. It was an interesting and enlightening experience to describe myself by what I did rather than who I worked for.

For Sophie, it was her prospective clients who made her think about her work in a different way. 'I don't need a full-time CFO, but I could do a day a week,' one of them said to her. Her first reaction was, *Why would I do that?* but when another business owner told her something similar, she started to think about serving multiple clients.

Getting clear about the value you already possess and that you can offer potential clients is key to making this transition. Nancy put it like this: 'I might not look like them and I might not be part of that gang anymore, but I can still do the same thing and I can actually do it better because I've done all these other things.'

One interviewee talked about building up the 'confidence that I am worthy of people's attention as a human being.' They described needing experience and self-awareness to come to this realisation. 'The armour of corporate stuff – the Big Four brand, the assets, the other teams and people – that's just stuff. I am worthy of this and places like where I worked are designed to make you think you're not, even if they would never phrase it that way!'

You're part of the team

If you're used to operating as part of a team, the thought of starting out on your own might be terrifying. Nobody to back you up, nobody to bounce ideas around with. One of my interviewees told me, 'I like being part of a team. I like firing hundreds of questions at them and having this big sounding board. And now it's just me.'

For another interviewee, it's led to a lot of conflicting emotions. 'I'm struggling with the sense of being alone,' they told me. 'I find myself feeling envy when I see people doing something really exciting in a team.' But they said that this feeling didn't take away from the strong sense they have 'that I need to define who I'm going to be, and I have to make my own path.'

Although your manager or other colleagues may be a reason for you to consider leaving, having them there to support and back you up may also give you pause. Katy appreciated the quality assurance of having someone within her team read her reports before they go out to clients, 'I'm losing the resource of the team, that second pair of eyes,' she said.

While you probably have an infrastructure supporting you currently – people and resources – it's important to figure out how much of it is needed on day one of your new venture for you to add value to your clients. Think about who you might be able to collaborate with and how you might organise things differently. Getting really clear about your strengths and weaknesses, where to put your focus and where to ask for help, will be key to your success. In Chapter 5 (Flow), we'll look at how to see your own value, what you might find easy and what you might struggle with.

You're not comfortable putting yourself out there

Running your own business means doing your own business development and your own sales, at least to begin with. It means putting yourself out there, and that's not comfortable for most people.

'What if people don't like me or the way I do things?'

'Do I have to share all my holiday videos or pictures of my lunch?'

'Will people judge me and how will I deal with that?'

Many people, including me, experience some level of doubt about their ability to succeed. Some have reservations, while others face a genuine fear of failure. One interviewee described it as 'a fear of being a small fish in a big competition.' They said, 'I'm choosing lack of financial stability, not having a support network around me, and no one to be able to share the workload with.'

Putting yourself out there and accepting that you might fail is part of running your own business. But there are definitely some parts of working for yourself that can feel scarier than others. Nancy said she used to think about business development as 'going out there and talking to strangers, which for most of us is the most terrifying thing in the world.' She's already thinking about new products and services she might offer her clients and told me, 'That's going to bring a level of vulnerability.'

Not everybody is going to like what you say and how you say it. In fact, if you're pleasing everyone, you're not doing things right! In Chapter 9 (Digital), we'll look at how to use the digital world to your advantage and in ways that feel authentic to you.

You don't think you're credible

If you're already being charged out by your current employer, this might not be an issue for you, but many people question if they'll be credible on the 'outside'. That thought can weigh heavy.

Justin described the importance of understanding and acknowledging our own fears. 'There's a significant potential for shame. You're putting yourself out there. I can talk a good game, but can I walk it?'

It's natural to worry about qualifications. Of course, it depends on your industry – some clients may ask you. But no one has ever asked about my coaching qualification or my qualifications to run people and culture workshops or to advise on all aspects of running and scaling a business. I'd be happy to share the details of course, but in my experience, prospective clients are much more interested in hearing about the other clients I've worked with and how I've solved their problems.

Tamara acknowledged her fears around legitimacy. 'Am I honestly qualified to do this, to charge clients for projects? Will people believe me? Am I the expert I'm claiming to be?'

Nancy told me her biggest fear was that people wouldn't want to work with her. She said that the fear of rejection was far bigger and more genuine than not making any money. 'Why would people want to work with me?'

It took me a while to understand the value of what I do and how best to package it. I had some uncomfortable moments along the way, especially when other people were seeing something I wasn't.

My story: 'It's a question of packaging it right.'

You know that feeling when you're not quite getting something? I was in a room with a few others sitting round a big boardroom table and I felt like I'd just failed some sort of test. All eyes were on me.

'I'm really not sure I'm ready just yet – all I have is a concept. I have no idea if anyone'll buy it...' I stammered.

The workshop leader looked at me quizzically. 'Is it the same skillset, the same intellectual property that you've used in your previous roles?'

I was confused. I can only do what I do. What else could it be? I felt myself getting hot and bothered. 'Yes. I think so,' I muttered, not knowing if that was the right answer and kicking myself for getting into this position.

It was the follow-up to the entrepreneurial event and I was there for two reasons. First, I was intrigued to understand their process. The next step was for them to try and sell me something, and I was intrigued to see how it worked. Plus, my husband and I were considering moving to the US and I wanted to understand what their presence was in that part of the world. What

I hadn't counted on was being asked such searching questions and feeling (again) like I was completely out of my depth.

'Lisa,' he said gently, 'People are already paying you lots of money for what you do. If you're planning to put these same skills to use, then it's a question of packaging it right and that's what we're here for.'

It's hard to explain the power of the epiphany I had in that moment. I had a set of skills. I'd already proved myself. People were already paying. Yes, there was lots to figure out, but I wasn't starting from scratch.

Leaving a well-known brand behind can be daunting. Several years after leaving employment, Andy was encouraging a former colleague to do the same. The response 'I couldn't do what I do without the big brand behind me' made him realise that he'd had a similar fear. But Andy had bolstered his credibility by associating his new business with a large brand whose products his team are specialists in implementing.

You're unsure of your identity

It's not just credibility that's a question when leaving behind a good, strong career in a large, well-known company. Many people also struggle with questions around identity. If you've seen yourself in a certain way for many years, it can be scary to think about fundamentally changing that. One interviewee told me their biggest fear was: 'Finding myself irrelevant and an island. Would I find belonging and meaning and good working relationships in my new life?'

There are also practical considerations. Even if you get help from the start, there are still many new things that every new business owner needs to get their head around. 'All my questions were practical,' one client told me during our interview. 'Without a massive company behind me, can I do all those little bits? Do I have those skills?'

Just like not being able to see our own value, the thought of having to sell yourself and win business might be terrifying. Not many of us are natural-born salespeople and yet as a business owner, you're always selling. The first person you'll need to sell yourself to is *you*, because if you don't believe in yourself, then you can't expect anyone else to. In Chapter 8 (Explore), we'll look at how to find your first few clients.

Leaving could come at a high price

One of the myths of entrepreneurship is the overnight success, the unicorn, the easy startup. But equally misleading and even damaging is the mantra of going all-in, working 24/7 and putting everything on the line. The price that entrepreneurs and business owners pay may well make you pause.

Didrik believes that every business owner should consider how they feel about the worst-case scenario. He told me a story about an entrepreneur from his native Sweden who asked himself, *'Am I OK to live in a tent in the forest?'* His answer was 'yes', and so he ploughed every penny into creating the high-performance car brand Koenigsegg. Most people are not prepared to be homeless and so Didrik's advice is to consider that it might not work out as expected, to understand your own limits and set appropriate boundaries.

Justin had run a business before, so had to think long and hard before starting out on his own again. 'I lost my marriage over it and almost became bankrupt. I came out with nothing other than a whole heap of learning and a whole lot of experience.' He had to be really sure that he was ready for the responsibilities that come with running your own business. 'Am I ready to go back there? Do the rewards outweigh the downsides?' For him the answer was clear.

Although we're talking a lot about freedom and doing your own thing, working for yourself and running a business is tough. During our interview, Tamara told me about wrestling with the decision to go for it. 'Everyone says that starting a business is super difficult. You have to work a hell of a lot. I know I can do it, but I like an easy life sometimes.'

Austin cautions that sacrifices need to be made in terms of relationships and free time. 'People who dislike pressure and enjoy doing what they want, when they want, need to be prepared for a major and possibly uncomfortable transition.' But, if successful, 'the sense of achievement, fulfilment and freedom can be tremendous.'

It's not only your own perception of the choice you're making that matters, but how others see it. Dealing with the fears and opinions of the people you care about can be a challenge. Nancy talked about the 'backlash' that some professionals, particularly in the legal profession, are experiencing when they're 'coming out and going on their own and being authentic.' She described how hard it is to break the mould and let go of the professional label. 'To break your parents' heart about the fact that their daughter isn't a lawyer anymore. It's hard and you carry that.' She explained the struggle of recognising you're capable of continuing along a certain path, but knowing it's not the right 'fit' for you.

If you make this change, you may find that some people can't accept your decision. 'Some just won't be onside,' Anish told me. You may even have to change your circle of friends because you're not accepted anymore.

'I'm not one of them anymore,' Nancy said. Ultimately, you're making a different choice from the one many people do, and some will find that challenging to deal with.

'Be prepared for some relationships to change,' Austin told me. 'Avoid discussing plans excessively with others: spend time on achieving results instead. Above all, be confident in yourself.'

CHAPTER 4

The Decision-Making Process

'In a world deluged by irrelevant information, clarity is power.'
— Yuval Noah Harari, Israeli historian[8]

We're all so different. Some people like to really mull a decision over a long period of time and others are more 'go with their gut' types. One interviewee told me they couldn't really get clear about anything while they were still working. 'All I was clear on was getting out,' they said. 'I had a broad direction of the types of work I was going to do and my first piece of client work lined up. That's all I knew.'

It can take time to figure out what you want. 'You think you know,' they told me. 'But actually, all you want is not to be in the corporate world anymore!'

---

8 YN Harari, *21 Lessons for the 21st Century* (Jonathan Cape, 2018)

What does success look like?

Do you feel successful? Do other people think you're successful?

There are many ways to measure success and it's important to understand which ones are important to you while considering the decision ahead.

Money: In many ways, this is the simplest of measures. Do you make more than you spend? Is there enough left over at the end of the month to be able to invest in things that are important to you? Are you able to provide for the people you love? Do you earn what you believe you're worth?

People: Are you able to have a positive impact on people's lives? Are you able to provide expertise, support and guidance to others? Whether it's clients, co-workers or members of your community, are you interacting and collaborating in ways you find fulfilling?

Impact: Do you make a difference in the world? Are you doing work you find meaningful? Are you working with people who inspire and motivate you because of the impact they're having? Does what you do matter? Is leaving a legacy important to you?

Learning: Are you growing and developing your skills and experience? Do you have the opportunity to explore, to have successes and failures, to learn? Are you able to play to your strengths and harness those of the people around you?

Satisfaction: Are you happy? Being happy isn't the same as settling for what you have. You can be happy and still want to achieve more! Does your work inspire you and make you want to get out of bed in the morning? Do you feel fulfilled and engaged and motivated?

Time: Are you in charge of your own time? Are you spending your time on what you want to be doing? Are you able to determine what you do and don't do? Do you have choices? Are you free to make your own decisions?

Whichever of these measures resonates with you, the point is that your view is the only one that counts. Comparing yourself with others is a waste of time, because they have a different definition of success from you. And they're making different choices from the ones you are.

I was reminded of this recently during a conversation with a friend. She was comparing her business with mine. I'd seen huge growth in the past few months, almost finished writing this book and started working with a new entrepreneurial accelerator programme. She was comparing herself negatively with me.

I pointed out that it was a false comparison. She has two children, a new partner and elderly parents with health issues, and she's made different choices. Her business is completely different from mine.

Measuring success is a deeply personal thing. And just looking at *outputs* is far too narrow a view. It's about what we choose to put our energy into.

If 50% of one person's energy is going into their business and someone else is giving 80% of theirs, is it fair to compare them? As we work our way through the next section of this book, keep in mind that chasing someone else's version of success is a waste of your time and energy. Whether you decide to leave employment and start your own business or not, your own personal measure of success is the only one that's relevant.

Self-doubt

Even if you're clear about what you want, how do you deal with all the doubt – that crushing feeling of dread and smallness? Have you ever noticed the narratives that run in your head? Those things you tell yourself about yourself that you'd never say out loud? The question I want to ask you is, 'How true are they, really?'

So much of what's going on in our brain is below the surface, but it has a huge impact on how we feel about ourselves and our businesses. Confidence is key in business, so let's make sure we're not making things harder for ourselves.

Scientists at Yale University followed a group of adults for twenty years to uncover the secret to a long life. What they discovered was ground-breaking. People who had a positive view of ageing in midlife lived an average of 7.6 years longer than those who had a negative view.[9] In other words, if you say, 'I think getting older is going to be great,' you're likely to live 7.6 years longer than your friend who says, 'I think getting older is going to be rubbish.'

Are you going to start your new business? Is your marriage going to make it through a rough patch? Is your company going to hit its projections for the year? The single biggest predictor for all these events is not the facts of your situation, but the story you tell. Many research studies have proved the life-changing magic of a productive story.[10]

The bad news is that negative stories are all around us – in the media, in society, in the thoughts our brains pop into our heads every now and then. The good news is that we have the power to change our own

---

9   Levy, BR, Slade, MD, Kunkel, SR, Kasl, SV, 'Longevity increased by positive self-perceptions of aging', *J Pers Soc Psychol*, 2002, 83(2), 261–70, https://pubmed.ncbi.nlm.nih.gov/12150226

10 Chen, L, Bae, SR, Battista, C, et al., 'Positive attitude toward math supports early academic success: Behavioral evidence and neurocognitive mechanisms', *Psychological Science*, 2018, 29(3), 390–402, https://journals.sagepub.com/doi/full/10.1177/0956797617735528

narrative. The *great* news is that it's not as hard as you might think. Small shifts in mindset can start a chain reaction of profound changes.

A dear friend of mine hit rock-bottom in her relationship. She feared it was going to end and became full of anxiety, guilt and shame. A chance conversation led her to read up on codependency. She learned that codependent relationships are far more than the 'clinginess' that is often an early signal. One partner needs the other partner, who in turn needs to be needed. This can become an unhealthy circular relationship which impacts the self-esteem and self-worth of the partner who is choosing to sacrifice themselves for the other person. She realised that instead of a mutually beneficial relationship, where both parties get their needs met, she was in danger of becoming the codependent party in an unhealthy partnership.

She took a long, hard look in the mirror and initiated some tough conversations with her partner. The changes that occurred in her life over the next few months were nothing short of miraculous. Not only did her relationship undergo profound positive change, but she also started having major breakthroughs in her business. Once she was able to acknowledge the importance of getting her own needs met, she was able to apply what she was learning to all areas of her life – personal and business. The clarity she continues to enjoy is inspiring, and came about all because she changed the narrative. What she believes about herself has fundamentally changed.

Our personal narratives are the stories we tell about ourselves. Many of them are drawn from our histories, the way we grew up, the decisions we made, the trajectories our lives have taken. Many also derive from fragments of our self-perception and the way we present ourselves.

The things you tell yourself about yourself, both silently and out loud, have a significant impact on what you believe. And our beliefs are the foundation of our behaviours. I often hear people saying things like, 'I'm not good with numbers, I can't sell, I'm too busy, lazy, stupid [etc],' and these things are said as if they're facts, rather than a narrative.

As with so many of the things, clarity is crucial. Once you identify the ideas, beliefs and convictions you're carrying, you can change them. Here are some tips to help.

Six tips: overcoming negative self-talk

1. Stop consuming negativity

We consume a terrifying amount of information every day and much of it is negative rubbish. A lot of what we find on social media is bad for us. Clickbait headlines are designed to stir our emotions. It's the equivalent of eating junk food, lots of calories with low nutritional value. It's addictive, destructive and bad for our brains. If you want to improve the stories you tell yourself, reduce the amount of rubbish you're consuming.

2. Stop looking at the cars!

Twenty years ago, I learned to ride a motorcycle. My boyfriend at the time was a keen motorcyclist and we decided to ride around the world on motorbikes. I enrolled on a four-day course to learn to ride, and on the first day they got us riding around a car park. The next day was out on the road and the advice they drummed into us was that the bike would follow our eyes – so we *had* to look at where we were going, at the traffic ahead of us, the obstacles we needed to navigate. As we left the car park, we had to turn right onto a road that had cars parked all along its side. Instead of looking to my right and the road I wanted to ride along, I focused on the stationary car directly opposite me, the one I was extremely keen to avoid, and drove straight into it!

We tend to obsess over things we're afraid of, whether it's business failure or a difficult conversation with a team member. The problem is in life, as when riding a motorcycle, we go where our focus goes. When you tell yourself lots of stories about how bad things are likely to be, you literally make that bad thing more likely to happen.

This is also the key to changing the pattern – see the road, not the cars. Instead of obsessing over the things that could go wrong, focus on the things that could go right. Tell stories, to your team and your family and in your own head, about the open road ahead of you. We have a natural tendency to look at the obstacles. Build a habit of looking at the road.

3. Change the narrative

Often the things we tell ourselves are simply not true. You might not be able to do advanced calculus in your head, but if you'd stop telling yourself that you can't do maths, for just five seconds, you could probably add those two numbers together without using a calculator.

Clinging to excuses like you're 'not a numbers person' or 'totally disorganised' has two dangerous consequences. First, it creates a compulsion to beat yourself up over something that really doesn't merit a self-flagellation session. Second, it prevents you from being able to do the thing you would otherwise be able to do if you weren't so busy telling yourself you couldn't do it.

How much of a relief would it be to know that you in fact *are* capable, you *are* valuable, you *are* strong, and you *are* able to do the things you want to do? The thing is, you already can. You just need to stop telling yourself you can't and start doing it.

Here's a great question to ask yourself: 'What evidence do I have for this narrative? How can I be certain that what I'm telling myself, about myself, is actually true?'

Listen out for things you frequently tell yourself and others that aren't uplifting or don't make you feel good about who you are. If you're stuck on this, ask a close friend if they've observed you putting yourself down or being unnecessarily hard on yourself. Once you're aware of the negative self-talk you can call it out. Challenge yourself instead. 'I'm not lazy. I'm choosing to spend my time another way.' What's the new truth you want to tell yourself instead?

Let me give you an example…

Many entrepreneurs feel that they never have enough time to do the things they need to do, let alone the things they want to do. And it's true, most business owners do have a lot to do. But it's all too easy to find yourself saying 'I have no time, I'm too busy' so often that it becomes oppressive. The more you say you don't have time, the more pressure you feel to work harder, make more, be more efficient – essentially, be better.

Once you realise the damage your 'no time' story is doing to your psyche – not to mention your family, your relationships and your health – you can decide to make a change. The first thing you can do is stop yourself from saying it all the time, and with such a stressed-out emphasis. You can replace 'I don't have time for that' with 'I'm not able to do that right now, but here's what I can do.'

Observe yourself throughout the day to find any inefficiencies in how you do things. Ultimately, time management is about the choices you make. Remove the stress from your shoulders and instead be kind to yourself and make decisions that are going to support your progress instead of making you feel bad.

4. Embrace the bumps in the road

One of my favourite stories as a child was *Pollyanna*, who always saw the positive and good in everything. Adults are harder to convince, and it's critical that the new narrative or story you tell yourself is true. If you're trying to convince yourself that losing weight or saving money is easy when it's not, you won't believe your own story. Denying reality doesn't work and will make you feel disconnected.

Instead of pretending everything's great when it's not, the trick is to accept what is happening and know that it will pass. Don't tell yourself a story about how easy or good things are. Instead tell yourself a story that says, 'This is all part of the plot.'

Every single success story has one thing in common – that moment when the hero needs to decide, against all odds, whether or not to keep going. It's important that we recognise that there will be bumps along the road to success. Instead of telling ourselves we're failing, we can remind ourselves that pushing through tough times is part of the process.

Research shows that when previously low-performing students are taught the growth mindset (we have to be bad at something for long enough to get good at it), their exam results improve.[11] Similarly, when you tell a team at the start of a project that failure is both inevitable and temporary, their likelihood of success increases.

It's important to accept the tough times in the knowledge that they will eventually pass. On most day, I'm a very positive person. My hormones are not! This means that fairly regularly, usually about once a month, I wake up feeling that nothing matters, nobody cares and everything is pointless. This used to knock me completely off balance, but I've learned to simply remind myself that this is normal for me and that it will pass. I'm able to keep going, even if I don't believe in what I'm doing for a day or two.

5. See the best in others

This is not just about your story but also the stories you tell about other people. Once again, the research

---

11 P Gouëdard, 'Can a growth mindset help disadvantaged students close the gap?', *PISA in Focus*, 2021, 112, https://doi.org/10.1787/20922f0d-en

here is clear. When teachers expect good things about their students, those students do better (even if the teachers don't say what they're thinking out loud).[12] The Pygmalion or Rosenthal effect holds that high expectations lead to improved performance.[13]

Stories change brains, and they change our behaviours. Practise telling good stories, even just in your own head, about your spouse, your team members and your clients. You'll find that when you change the story you're telling about them, they will change too.

6. Do one thing

When we feel overwhelmed, we try and think things through. We run scenarios in our head, we try and get clear, and we end up going round in circles. Still overwhelmed, still frustrated, still no further forward.

The answer to this is surprisingly simple. When you're feeling overwhelmed, take an action. Do one thing. It doesn't matter what it is! By taking action, you move your brain from thinking to doing. You literally reset your brain.

---

12 RC Pianta, 'Classroom management and relationships between children and teachers: Implications for research and practice', In CM Evertson and CS Weinstein (Eds.), *Handbook of Classroom Management: Research, practice, and contemporary issues* (Lawrence Erlbaum Associates Publishers, 2006), https://psycnet.apa.org/record/2006-01816-026

13 Duquesne University, 'The Pygmalion Effect', no date, www.duq.edu/about/centers-and-institutes/center-for-teaching-excellence/teaching-and-learning-at-duquesne/pygmalion

Research shows that when people with huge financial debts pay off their smallest bill right away, they are much more likely to ultimately become debt-free.[14] Think of the brain as a binary system: you're either frozen in fear or empowered by action. If you have a huge to-do list, check off the smallest thing first. Talk to one person, make one call. The chemicals in your brain will change, and so will your story.

The thought of setting up your own business might be daunting, but that's exactly why I wrote this book! Next, we'll look at the decision-making process. If you decide at the end of Part Two that this is the right decision for you, then Part Three is full of practical help on how to make your new business a success.

First, though, let's consider a possible step along the way.

Halfway

This book is focused on taking the journey all the way to starting your own business and serving multiple clients. But becoming a contractor or interim is an intermediate step that you could choose to take. It's still a full-time role and you're still reporting to

---

14 AL Brown, JN Lahey, 'Small victories: Creating intrinsic motivation in task completion and debt repayment', *Journal of Marketing Research*, 2015, 52(6), 768–783, https://journals.sagepub.com/doi/abs/10.1509/jmr.14.0281

someone else and doing things their way, but it can be a useful way of figuring out the mindset that's so key to being a successful business owner. It's a natural first step for many people and the way I made the transition from employee to self-employed myself.

Before we move on to Part Two, doing a simple pros and cons exercise will help you get clear about your current thinking.

PROS AND CONS

We've looked at many reasons why you might choose to leave employment or stay put. Your brain may be full of conflicting information, thoughts and feelings. Capturing these on paper will help you clear your mind and focus on what's going to work for you.

Get out a piece of paper (or a screen if you prefer) and draw a line down the middle from top to bottom. On one side, write down all the reasons why you want to make a change, why working for yourself is right for you. And on the other side of the page, write down all the reasons why not.

Didrik advises, 'If you're the type of person that tends to regret your decisions, keep this list!'

Once you've completed your pros and cons list, you can consider the different factors that will help you make your decision. Read on to find out more.

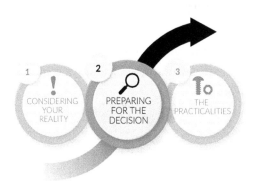

PART TWO

PREPARING FOR THE DECISION

In Part One of this book, we looked at some of the reasons why you may be thinking of making the move from employment to starting your own business. You listed out your pros and cons. Although you now have a clearer idea of how you feel, we need to gather together some data and insights to help inform your decision.

I'm delighted to share with you the FREEDOM Formula, which I use to guide my clients through the decision-making process. You may already be well on your way to choosing to start your own business but want some facts to back it up. Or you may be exploring a number of options and want to understand if starting up on your own would work for you. What you *do* know is that something needs changing in your life.

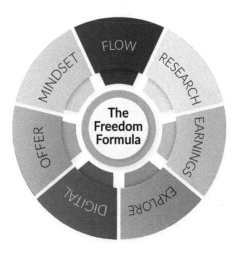

My model is called the FREEDOM Formula because freedom is exactly what it gives you. Freedom looks different to every single person. For some, it means financial security, for others the ability to plan their own time. For you, it may mean being able to balance the things you want to do. For me, it means being able to run my businesses from wherever I am in the world. Whatever freedom means to you, helping you get clear about whether or not starting your own business is right for you is the greatest gift I can give you. There's no right or wrong here. What's important is understanding what you want and what it would take to achieve it.

This part of the book looks at the different factors you'll want to weigh up as part of your decision-making process. We'll look at doing things your own way and getting into your flow. We'll talk about what research you need to do. We'll crunch some numbers and discuss how to harness your network. We'll delve into the digital world and answer your questions about how to structure and price your offerings, and we'll get your head in the right place to make this decision.

Each chapter will look in turn at the components of the FREEDOM Formula:

- Flow
- Research
- Earnings
- Explore
- Digital
- Offer
- Mindset

Be warned – there may be a part of your brain that's freaking out right now. I mentioned earlier that your brain's primary function is to keep you safe. It doesn't like change and as you go through this process, it may try to sabotage you. It may introduce self-doubt ('Who do you think you are?') or it may try to distract you with lots of urgent but unimportant things to do, like checking your social media or getting really busy at work. Or it may tell you that you're really tired and can think about all this tomorrow.

My advice is not to try and ignore that piece of your brain that's fearful and desperately trying to keep you safe. Instead, be kind to yourself. Tell yourself it's OK. You understand that part of you may be scared. Try gentle reasoning and negotiation. Tell your brain that you haven't yet made your decision and that what you're doing by reading this book is exploring your options and gathering information. Part Two of this book covers the different aspects you need to know, find out or consider as you move towards the time when you'll decide. Make sure your brain understands we're not there yet.

CHAPTER 5

Flow – Doing Things Your Way

'Success is liking yourself, liking what you do and liking how you do it.'
— Maya Angelou, American poet[15]

One of the strongest motivations people have for transitioning from employment to running their own business is wanting to do things their own way. Maybe you're sick of someone looking over your shoulder or second-guessing your decisions, or perhaps you've got some ideas about how to shake up your industry that you're itching to try out.

Nancy talked about 'shaking off what you're supposed to do and doing what you feel like you want to be doing, what makes you feel good.' She told me it's about authenticity. 'For the first time in my life I feel

---

15 *Pocket Maya Angelou Wisdom: Inspiring quotes and wise words* (Hardie Grant Books, 2019)

like I'm reaching my potential. I am doing what flows. I haven't had a day yet that's felt hard.'

One of the crucial things to consider as you weigh up this decision is understanding what gives you energy and what drains it. In this chapter, we'll look at what we mean by 'doing things your way', and we'll explore what you might find easy and difficult about working for yourself and running your own business.

Your energies

It's human nature to be curious about other people and quite natural to compare ourselves with them. It's one of the ways we learn. As babies, we mimic what we see. As children, we look at older children and also at our parents for indicators on how we should behave. We're looking for guidance on how to do something we don't know yet how to do. We accept that we have to try things before we can master them.

Something seems to get lost in translation as we grow into teenagers and start adhering to social norms. Instead of looking at something and saying, 'How would I do that in my way?', we're more likely to try and copy something or someone exactly and then beat ourselves up for not immediately being able to do it as well. We ignore the fact that the person we're looking at and comparing ourselves to is different from us. They're wired differently and they have different perspectives and experience.

I can trace my relationship with energy all the way through my career. Especially in those moments when I've formed strong partnerships with some great bosses, who to this day I still feel enormously privileged to have worked with. Throughout my career, I've experienced the magic that happens when an ambitious, impatient, creative person meets someone like me, who's a natural implementer.

The importance of energy in building fantastic teams and sustainable businesses really landed for me when I started working with entrepreneurs and their teams. I got involved in the development of a psychometric profiling tool that helps people understand what gives them energy and what drains it. I use it to help business owners get the best from their people and build strong, collaborative and productive teams.

What I see is many people comparing themselves with others without asking themselves the fundamental question: 'How could I do this in a way that would work for me?'

My story: 'Why would you want to be as good as me?'

I discovered the power of this question quite by accident. In March 1996, on my very first day at Xerox, I was shown round the office and introduced to the sales team. I remember one man being especially welcoming with a big smile and lots of chat. He had certificates up on the cabinet next to his desk, prizes he'd won as a salesperson and photographs of him in exotic locations receiving trophies from the managing director. I was impressed and more than a little intimidated. When I saw a certificate dated the year I was born, it totally blew my mind. *I want to be as successful as him!* I thought.

I started my sales career in a new telesales team. Our job was to call schools and colleges across the south of England to let them know Xerox had just secured a huge contract with their local council. This meant excellent deals on new photocopiers and lots of opportunities to upgrade. There were four of us: Jim, Aidan, Nick and me. A great team with lots of potential and only one problem. Me.

I was horrified to discover that I was absolutely terrified of cold calling. I just couldn't get my head around it. I hated 'disturbing' people, a feeling that came across loud and clear to the people on the other end of the phone. I found myself doing everything I could to avoid picking up the phone. I made myself useful to my manager and teammates, offering to print reports and collate results. It soon became clear that I wasn't making as many calls as the others were. I hated my job and I was rubbish at it.

The smiley salesman who'd been so welcoming on my first day found me outside one morning, head in hands, hiding in a corner. My job was turning into a nightmare. I knew they'd have to fire me if I didn't improve. I felt so ashamed. 'I can't believe I'm blowing this,' I moaned. 'My dream job, straight out of university, with such an amazing company.' I felt like such a failure. He tried to comfort me, but I was having none of it. I was intent on indulging in a full-on pity party! 'I'll never be as good as you!' I threw at him.

He just looked at me with his kind, twinkly eyes. Then he stood up and as he walked away, he asked over his shoulder, 'Why would you want to be as good as me, when you can be as good as you?'

I decided to write a letter to my potential clients introducing myself, explaining the deals on offer and telling them I would call them to discuss their options. It worked a treat. I still didn't like the cold calling, but it was *so* much easier to say I was calling about a letter I'd written. The conversations flowed, I felt much more natural, and the sales started to follow.

As you consider whether to start your own business, it's important to get clear about what doing things your own way actually means. What would you do differently from your current employer? Which aspects of what your clients will want from you are you going to enjoy, and which tasks will be more of a chore?

How to make things work for you

You're considering a big change to your life, and you're likely to find some elements of it easier than others. Different people find certain things challenging and others easy. Understanding how you're wired is vital. By that, I mean what gives you energy and what drains it. When I talk about 'flow', I'm referring to your natural energies. According to the tool I use to help clients with this, we all have different amounts of four different energies. They determine how we see the world, how we interact with others, how we make decisions and what kind of businesses we build.

There's the **activating** energy, which is full of ideas and drive and ego and innovation. Head in the cloud and always looking to the future. This energy likes change and taking risks and is always looking to mix things up. You need this energy to start a business.

There's the counterbalancing **sustaining** energy, which is grounded in the here and now. With a focus on balance and avoiding conflict, this is a more reflective energy that we need to bring consistency to our businesses.

Then there's the **inspiring** energy, which is all about the people. Collaborating, engaging and connecting with others is what this energy is all about and we need this to bring team members on board, manage our clients and engage with investors.

Last but by no means least, there's the **refining** energy, which focuses on *how* to get things done. Structure and facts and numbers – we need this energy to build systems and processes so that we can scale and make some money!

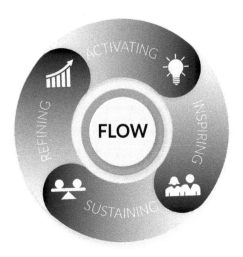

The tool I use helps you understand how much of each of these energies you have. It's a key enabler to finding your individual flow as well as the flow of the people around you – your future clients, partners and team members. It changes the way people see themselves and how they approach building and running a business.

Finding your flow is a constant process of trying different things and finding what works for you. It comes from looking at what you're spending your time and focus on. It increases your awareness of where you get your energy from and what drains it.

If you're full of drive and innovation, you'll need to bring creativity to everything you do. You'll probably find too many structured admin tasks draining, so you'll need to find ways of approaching them so they're challenging and therefore more palatable to you. Mix it up, set yourself goals, make it interesting.

Routines and processes will help you stay focused if consistency, balance and harmony are important to you. Ask yourself who could help you put these in place. Be kind to yourself and encourage yourself to push boundaries and try new things. Keep track of the progress you're making and reward yourself for a job well done.

If you get your energy from being around others, then everything you do needs to be collaborative. Who could you work with on each piece of your new business? What can you do for someone else so that they will be able to spend time with you tackling the tasks you keep putting off? How can you introduce more fun and variety into your day?

You may find dealing with lots of people drains your energy, if focusing on completing tasks is what drives you. You'll need to plan your time accordingly. I love running workshops, but I always block my calendar out afterwards so I can decompress and recharge my batteries. Practise talking about how you feel and take pride in your ability to bring order to chaos.

It's important to understand that your 'wiring' or preferences are not the same as your capabilities. You're extremely capable of doing anything you set your mind to. You just need to do it in ways that work for you. If you decide to venture out on your own, you're going to want to build a team around you. This will enable you to spend all of your time in your flow. But until then, focus on doing things in ways that are not going to drain you.

OVER TO YOU: REVIEW YOUR TIME

Before moving on to the next chapter, take a look at your calendar for the last couple of weeks. What did you find energising and when were you tired? Try to identify those tasks or activities that you find draining and which light you up. How could you change your approach or schedule to spend more of your time in your flow?

CHAPTER 6

Research – What's The Market Telling You?

'Research is formalized curiosity. It's poking and prying with a purpose.'
— Zora Neale Hurston, American anthropologist[16]

Although doing things your way is often a strong motivator, that doesn't mean that you shouldn't do your research. If nothing else, it will reassure the fearful part of your brain that you're making an informed decision. Talk to people in your network, gather inputs, insights and information. It will be invaluable in helping inform your decision.

Tamara was a culture consultant about to leave her job. She talked about dreaming big but doing her research. 'Get your ducks in a row as far as possible.' She told me how generous people had been with their time,

---

16 Zora Neale Hurston, *Dust Tracks on a Road* (J. B. Lippincott, 1942)

even strangers she had contacted via their websites to ask for advice. 'So many have spoken with me about their own experiences, offered advice and put me in touch with people in their network with nothing in return but my effusive thanks!' The resounding message she got from those conversations is that nobody regretted making the transition to doing their own thing, although some wished they'd done more planning and built up a savings pot so they didn't have to start 'paddling like a duck on speed from day one.' She's been learning and networking and absorbing as much as possible in preparation for taking the plunge.

In this chapter, we'll look at a key area of your research – your market. Who's in your space and what are they doing? What kind of business might you set up if you decide to go that route?

Assessing the market

You need to understand if there's space for you in your market. As you're currently employed in this space, it's safe to assume that there are clients to be won. Let's not get hung up about *how* to win them yet, but we need to be sure that the market is there.

This is important because it's all too easy to get caught up in the excitement of new opportunities. Anish told me that he made the mistake of listening to too many influencers. 'There's a kind of "build it and they will come" type fantasy that happens when you first start out. Because you're so enthusiastic, you feel you're being spoken to directly. I was so enamoured by the idea that I didn't stop to think about what I was doing.'

Can you find data on the size of your market? Are there people who have the problems you want to solve? Are these problems painful enough that they're willing to pay to solve them?

It's a good idea to check out the competition, if only to be aware of who's doing what in your space. You'll need to understand who and what potential clients may be comparing you with. Your current employer is likely to be your competitor, but don't let that put you off. We're in research mode for now. Take an objective look at what they are doing and how. Who is in your industry? Are there established businesses? What about other single operators?

Use this simple set of questions to help you research the various players in your space.

Tool – Competitive analysis

- What size of company are they (how many people)?

- What kind of clients do they serve?

- How do they attract their clients?

- What services do they offer?

- How do they price them?

- What do they do well?

- What could they do better?

- What are the main differences between them and you?

Competitive analysis can be scary but remember, we're just doing research here. Remind yourself that all these businesses and people you're looking at were once in your shoes. Everyone starts at the beginning.

One of my interviewees told me about their policy of making friends with their competitors. 'It's part of my job to have formal discussions with the opposites in my legal cases,' they told me. 'Building relationships is so important.'

If you're worried about competing with established businesses, remember that some people like the assurance of working with an established company that has a whole team of people who can support them, while others prefer the flexibility, responsiveness and personal touch of working directly with an expert like you.

When Didrik started his business, they were a team of five. 'When we pitched to clients, we often felt that it was a weakness that we weren't bigger,' he told me. 'Later, we realised that it was actually part of our USP [unique selling point]. Our clients could easily get in direct contact with senior members of the team, and we were able to customise our offerings in ways that our larger competitors were not.'

The crucial thing to remember is that in any market of a decent size, there are enough clients to go around. You won't appeal to everyone and nor would you want to. We'll talk about this more in later chapters.

Finding your space

We're all unique. Nobody else has your exact experience, perspective or way of doing things. You may find there's a gap in the market that you can step into and make your own. Perhaps nobody else is combining skills in the particular way you do or approaching problems with the solution you have. If this is the case for you, think of a way of describing what you do that makes your uniqueness clear.

Nancy is combining her legal, commercial and construction knowledge to carve out a space of her own. 'Things need not be difficult' is her strapline. It speaks to her potential clients who avoid reading contracts and see commercial negotiations as challenging.

With any kind of change comes opportunity, and you may be able to benefit. Tamara has identified a gap in the market around turning cultural insights into concrete actions. She'll be working with companies who want to take a step forward regarding culture, perhaps because they're moving into new markets or having to adjust to new channels, but need some help with what that means practically. 'People read an article online saying you need to be culturally sensitive when you move into new markets,' she told me. 'But what does that actually mean? How do I do that?' Her focus will be on helping companies turn good intentions into executable strategies.

Bear in mind that you may not be able to see exactly what sets you apart, so it can be extremely valuable to talk this through with people you trust to give you objective inputs. When Andy was considering leaving employment, he was thinking of himself as a 'project manager' until I pointed out that he was operating in a specialist area. 'Realising I had a specialism made a big difference to me,' he said.

OVER TO YOU: ASSESSING YOUR MARKET AND YOUR PLACE IN IT

Let's pause a moment and recap on what you've discovered so far. What does your market look like and where's the space for you? What problems are being solved and who's doing what? Who are the players and what makes you different?

CHAPTER 7

Earnings – Know Your Numbers

'If you don't know your numbers, you don't know your business.'

— Marcus Lemonis, Lebanese-born businessman[17]

Financial security is a big factor when considering the leap to entrepreneurship. It's vital to know your numbers before making any decisions. Think carefully about your finances and be realistic about what you want and what's achievable. Consider building a financial reserve and a contingency plan in case things don't go according to plan. Your attitude towards money will likely depend on your personal situation, for example if you have family members to support or debts to pay. 'Don't do it at the financial

---

17   K Elkins, 'Marcus Lemonis outlines the 3 numbers every business leader should know', CNBC, 2016, www.cnbc.com/2016/08/29/the-profit-star-marcus-lemonis-financial-numbers-to-know.html

risk of your family,' Nancy told me. 'Know what your financial limits are.'

One of the mistakes you want to avoid is making a direct comparison between your salary when employed and what you could earn 'on the outside'. You need to consider not just what you can earn but also what it's going to cost you to earn it. In this chapter, we'll look at how to understand your base case, what costs you need to understand and how to plan out different scenarios.

Base case and buffer

Let's first work out your base case. What do you need to take home to maintain your desired lifestyle? Nothing extravagant, no expensive holidays or fancy clothes (yet). Put another way, what level of earnings would you be prepared to put up with to start this new venture?

Many people have no idea what they spend in an average month. If that's you, I suggest you change your perspective, for two reasons. First, you cannot make an informed decision about whether to leave employment without understanding your numbers. And second, if you do decide to start your own business, you'll need to know and manage your finances.

Once we understand your base case, we need to look at how much buffer you're comfortable with. How many months of money do you need in your bank account? Comfortable is a relative term, of course. A certain level of discomfort is necessary to take the plunge, but what we don't want is you freaking out and not being able to think clearly. A degree of anxiety is quite normal when running your own business. It's important that you're honest with yourself about what you can manage.

The buffer calculation will be different for each person and will be impacted by your relationship with risk. It will also depend on your individual circumstances, for example, if you have dependents to support or debts to pay off. Think of it as a runway: how long do you need it to be? Take what you have in the bank and divide it by what you need to live on per month. How do you feel about that number? For most people, I recommend having enough in the account to cover three to six months' worth of your living costs.

Costs

One of the key pieces of research you'll need to do is to work out your likely costs. Here are some areas to consider to get you started.

Location and equipment: Where will you work from? You might not need an office, but you'll at least want a proper desk and chair. Consider the supplies and equipment you'll need. What about travel expenses? You'll probably need to use a few different pieces of software. Although each one on its own might cost a small amount, they soon add up when added together. Make sure you include these costs in your numbers.

Accountant: You're going to need an accountant, and I suggest identifying one early on, as they can be invaluable in advising you through this process. If you're someone who really doesn't like dealing with numbers, you may want an accountant who will also do bookkeeping for you and tell you what you can withdraw each month. Get some recommendations from people in your network, have some conversations and find out what it will cost if you decide to proceed.

Website: You're going to need a simple one-page website. Talk to people in your network and find out what this will cost to have built. In addition, you'll need a domain and an email address. We'll discuss these more in Chapter 9 (Digital). For now, just get a sense of the cost of building but also for hosting your website on an ongoing basis.

Coach: Several people I spoke to have the cost of a business coach in their budget. 'I don't see it as a luxury,' one interviewee told me. 'It was an essential part of my process.' They also shared with me that when they started seeing their coach, it wasn't to work through leaving their job. 'I went to whinge about my boss. At no point did my coach tell me to leave.' They told me that among all the options they discussed with their coach, the option to leave their job was the least favourite. 'I always pushed that away. I thought, *I'm just going to be strong, more confident, more assertive and then they'll know! Then he'll listen to me.*

Nancy has been a client of mine for over a year. She first came to me for help navigating her way through corporate life and ended up navigating her way out. She describes our monthly sessions as critical in 'keeping me honest.'

Insurance and health care: When you're considering costs, think about what your current employer covers. Do you have private health insurance, and what about your pension? Depending on your sector, you may need to take out professional indemnity insurance.

Professional development: Although you already have valuable skills and experience, you may decide that you want to improve on certain areas. I'd been coaching informally for years, but I got myself certified as a coach in my first year of business. Putting money in your budget for additional training as part of your transition plan can be a smart move. One word of warning though: learning can lead to procrastination. There's always more to learn and another course to enrol on. Don't let yourself get derailed by becoming a course junkie!

Taxes: Finally, don't forget that the tax authorities will want their cut before you're able to take any money out of your business. Your accountant will help you make some rough calculations.

Income

Now you know your base case, your buffer and your costs, it's time to map out your income. We'll look at what you're selling and how much to charge in more detail in Chapter 10 (Offer), but let's make some assumptions now.

- If you're currently working directly with clients, how much does your employer charge for your services?

- How long are the different kinds of engagements or projects you work on and how much do clients pay for them?

- How many hours do you want to work each week, or how many days in a typical month?

- How much time off are you planning for holidays or other activities?

Make some assumptions about how much you can charge. If you're being charged out by your current employer, I would estimate between 50% and 100% of that number. If not, then find out what people are paying for the type of services you're planning to offer. Consider the size of clients you'll be able to attract.

Katy and I spent several sessions together mapping out her numbers. 'Knowing how many jobs, what kind of jobs I needed to be doing – breaking that down really kept me focused, whereas before it seemed like a daunting task.'

It's important to be realistic but conservative in your estimates. Think about what you want your week to look like, but also what people will pay and how many clients you'll need to bring in the revenue you need.

OVER TO YOU: CREATE YOUR PLANNING SPREADSHEET

Before moving onto the next chapter, create a simple spreadsheet that lists all your costs, including your base case number.

Map how much you'll need to earn to make your numbers work and how often you'll need to sign a new client. Do a sense check on how many clients you can manage at any one time and remember that you'll need to spend time each week on non-client-facing activities.

Don't forget to factor in your buffer – the amount of money you need to see in the bank to avoid anxiety becoming a problem rather than a healthy motivator.

We'll do much more work on this in future chapters. For now, what you're trying to get a handle on is how viable your business would be and how realistic your expectations around earnings are.

CHAPTER 8

Explore – Your Network

'You can have everything in life you want if you will just help enough other people get what they want.'

— Zig Ziglar, American salesman and author[18]

One of the questions you may have in your head is, 'How will I find clients?' You're unlikely to take the plunge without identifying a few potential clients. Your network is an invaluable resource to leverage not only for insights and information but also for introductions, referrals and clients. In this chapter, we'll look at where your first clients will come from and how to test the waters with them.

---

18   Z Ziglar, *Secrets of Closing the Sale* (Berkley Books, 1984)

Your first client

It's extremely likely that your first client will be someone you already know or will be introduced to you by someone you know. Maybe it will be a former colleague, supplier or client. Perhaps a friend of a friend. They may not have to persuade you to do business with them as Philip did with me, but I have no doubt that they'll be just as insightful.

My story: 'I really think you can help me, Lisa!'

Philip is an amazing landscape architect. We met on a course for entrepreneurs where I was lucky enough to find myself on a table of experienced business owners. As well as Philip, there was a seasoned property developer; a serial entrepreneur; a man who ran a large jewellery business; a TV journalist who'd been running her communications company for many years; and a man who helps entrepreneurs raise capital. And then there was me. On the first day, the fundraising man asked me what I did. 'I help entrepreneurs scale their businesses,' I boldly told him, with more confidence than I felt inside.

'Oh, that's really interesting,' he replied. 'How do you do that?'

'That's what I'm here to figure out,' I muttered, feeling like a fraud.

I listened, I absorbed, and I persevered, even though I often felt like I had no clue what I was doing. In month two of the course, we learned about pitching our services and in month three, we started mapping out the book we wanted to write. That was when Philip asked me to lunch. He told me all about his business and his team and I asked him lots of questions. We started to explore some of his challenges and I confidently offered him my perspective.

I was shocked when he told me he'd like to engage my services to work with his team. I hadn't seen him as a potential client, and I was confused. This was somebody who'd watched me struggle to get clear about what I was doing and how to package it. He'd seen me flounder and doubt myself. All the confidence I'd been feeling drained away. How could I possibly help? What did I know?

'I'll put something together for you,' I said, trying to muster a confidence I certainly didn't feel.

When I got home, I made myself write my first proposal, which, to my surprise, he accepted. On my first visit to his office, I met with members of his team individually and asked them about the company. What was working well and what could be improved? What was it like working in this team and for this boss? One man asked me about my work, not realising that this was my first day at my first client. Suddenly, my confidence came flooding back. I *did* know what I was doing. I *do* know how to ask questions and cut through all the noise and get to the heart of the matter. I understand people and processes regardless of the size of the business.

Your first client will be a learning experience, so my advice is to choose them wisely. They will help you understand what works and what doesn't. It's very unlikely to be perfect, so try to start with someone who will give you honest feedback and allow you to evolve your offering.

Your network

Don't underestimate the power of the network you've built up during your career so far. One of the pieces of advice I give people at the beginning of their working lives is to connect with everyone you meet. You never know where they might end up, who you may be able to introduce each other to, or how you may be able to support each other in the future. 'Because I've really focused on nurturing relationships over the years and not asking for anything,' Katy told me, 'now that I'm going on my own, people in my network are really stepping up to support me without me even having to ask. I'm so grateful.'

When you think about your network, who do you know who might need your services? Who could you have an informal, off-the-record, hypothetical 'If I was to do this, would you be interested?' type of chat with?

Sophie's advice is: 'As soon as you quit, call everyone you know and tell them what you do!' That's certainly what I did, and I remember being surprised and gratified at how many people responded. People in my network continue to be incredibly supportive. I receive regular messages of support, referrals and introductions from people I haven't worked with or met in years. Often, it's people I don't know well, who I maybe met years ago and connected with on LinkedIn. Perhaps they've read my book, signed up for my weekly email or been reading one of my social media posts and one day they, or someone they know, need a business coach and they get in contact.

There are people you know who will likely jump at the chance of working with you, or at the very least want to support you by introducing you to people in their network. A great question to ask is: 'Who do you know who could benefit from a conversation with me?'

Anish shared with me that he wished he'd done more network-building before leaving his employer. 'I wish I'd developed more of a black book in terms of relationships and not felt fraudulent about getting in touch with old bosses.' He's learned a lot about reciprocity since he's been running his business and found that people are usually happy when you get back in touch.

He wishes he'd 'primed his network ahead of time' to let them know he was going independent.

Your current employer

One place you might not think to look for your first client is your current employer. I would advise you to read your contract carefully before informing them of your plans, but they may well be willing, if not eager, to hold on to you in some capacity. That was the case for Nancy, whose employer was keen to keep her on a part-time basis. Andy offered training services to his previous employer as a way of supplementing his income in his first years of business. And my first contract role was back at Xerox, the last place I'd have thought of returning to.

My story: 'Would you like to come back as a contractor or an employee?'

When I left Xerox, I had no intention of going back. I was done. But the world is a funny old place, and less than a year after I'd handed in my notice, I found myself in an unexpected situation. I'd moved on to a fantastic new job at a music company, where I was charged with deploying Lean Six Sigma to teams around the world. They were heavily invested in their new strategy, and I knew I could make a real impact. But only a few weeks in, my then boyfriend asked me, 'You remember that long-shot job I applied for, the one in the mortgage-backed securities team? I've just been offered it. Will you come with me?'

We headed to New York as the financial crisis was about to hit. My new husband even called his boss before we boarded the flight and asked him if we should still come. We were assured that the market could halve and halve again, and they'd still be OK. After a few crazy months, he went from working eighteen-hour days to having nothing to do. We knew our days in the United States were numbered. His visa was dependent on his job and mine was dependent on his. It was time to make a move. I hit the phones and made a call I never expected to make. The first person I reached out to was someone who'd tried to persuade me not to leave the previous year.

'I thought you guys were going for a few years,' he quipped.

'You and me both!' I replied.

If I hadn't been offered the choice of going back to Xerox as a contractor, I might never have started on this amazing road to entrepreneurship. Another person to be grateful to in a very long list, and a reminder never to burn bridges. The experience proved to be a real eye-opener for me. In many ways, I got the best of both worlds. I got to learn how to be a contractor while being treated as a well-respected colleague by people who'd worked with me previously. I got some distance and learned the right mindset.

It's important to learn as much as possible from the people you work with before you leave and keep in touch with them after you do. 'Don't cut anyone off,' one interviewee told me. 'Don't burn your bridges, you never know what's round the corner.'

I urge you to think carefully about how you'd like things to be structured. If your motivation is to serve several clients at the same time, as mine was, then consider this before signing up for a full-time contract with your current employer. It can be a bridge to the future you want, but what you need is more than simply changing the way you're paid.

OVER TO YOU: LEVERAGE YOUR NETWORK

Spend some time thinking about and talking to potential clients in your network. Who would be the top five to ten names on your list? Who do you know who could refer you to people who might need your services?

CHAPTER 9

Digital – Your Online Presence

'Let excellence be your brand.'
— Oprah Winfrey, American talk show host[19]

As we're discovering, there are many different facets to the decision about leaving employment and starting up your own business. This chapter looks at your brand and your online presence. We'll discuss what name to use, what needs to be on your first website and how to start out with social media.

This chapter is all about what you need to think about to get started. We'll look at how your presence in the digital world might evolve as your business grows in Part Three of this book.

---

19   O Winfrey, 'Let EXCELLENCE be your BRAND', www.youtube.com/watch?v=q08mUUxQoNw&t=124s

This is one area where it's easy to get overwhelmed. There's a lot to consider, but when we boil it down, to get started you'll need just four things: your brand, a one-page website, an email address and one social media profile.

Your brand

Your brand is who you are and what you stand for. It's the experience your clients have when working with you. It's what you want to say and how you choose to say it. It's not about fancy logos or fonts or design. Those things are outputs.

Working with a branding specialist early on will help you get really clear about your business and its values. Caroline, the owner and founder of Somer Design, talked to me about using the clarity and confidence that comes from having a distinct brand to build authority in your market. 'Having a distinct brand with clear messaging enables you to really cut through the crowd and stand out,' she told me.

The first thing to consider in the digital world is what name you're going to use. Are you going to use a separate brand name, or your own? You are the person with the skills, the contacts and the experience, so you may choose to use your own name, as I have. But what about if you choose to grow a team, or partner with others?

We'll talk later about different ways of growing and scaling your business and the pros and cons of each type of model. Using your own name can definitely limit your options, so think carefully about what's going to work for you.

The name you use doesn't necessarily have to be the same as your company name. In the UK, you're allowed to use a trading name as long as your company name appears on your invoices and website.

Website and email

To get started, you'll need a one-page website that clearly tells people what you do – and in some cases what you don't do. Simple works best here. You're at the beginning of your business journey and that's OK.

The reason for having a simple website from the start is that people will often want to check you out. If they've been referred by someone who knows you or has worked with you previously, they might want the bit of extra comfort that seeing a website gives.

Your website needs to clearly articulate who you are and what you do. It needs to spell out the problem you solve and who you solve it for. It also needs to cover how you do what you do and what makes you special. What's your angle, what makes you different, and why should people work with you? It needs a photo of you, and you want the site to look clean and professional. It should make it easy for people to understand your offering and how they can contact you.

You'll want to get an email address set up that links to your new domain. You'll also want to think about online security and protecting your information and that of your clients from online scammers and hackers. Francis, a cybersecurity expert, advises everyone to install good antivirus software and use two-factor authentication. Depending on your sector, you may need to think about more robust measures.

In terms of domain name, you have a few choices. You can go for your name, as I did with www.lisazevi.com, or the name of your company, as Austin did with www.edward-austin.com. If you're in a specialised niche, you could decide to go with a domain name related to what people will search for in Google, like Katy did with www.fairpayhub.co.uk. You can also choose to have several domain names all pointing at the same place.

There's no right or wrong here. My advice is to keep it simple. Many people, including me, have spent far too long and thrown far too much money down the digital rabbit hole!

Social media

Likewise, when you're starting out, my advice for social media is to keep it simple. Pick one channel and do it well. Do your research and think about where your potential clients are.

If you're coming from the corporate world, **LinkedIn** may be the most appropriate channel for you, depending on what services you're offering. It can be a great way to build connections and generate leads. **Instagram** works particularly well for people working in creative fields, especially highly visual areas like design as well as for physical products. An alternative channel that's used by millions for inspiration is **Pinterest**. If your goal is to build a community and connect people together, then **Facebook** may be the place to start, although this channel also works well for B2B (business to business) awareness. **Twitter** may be the channel for you if you're focused on sharing ideas and asking questions, whereas if you're looking to appeal to a younger demographic, you may choose to start on **TikTok**. If you're planning on sharing video content, **YouTube** may be the place for you, whereas **Snapchat** is used by brands to offer a more intimate and direct experience.

To start with, we're not thinking about posting. We're just getting you ready to put yourself out there. We'll talk about sales and marketing, including digital content, later in the book.

If you're using a channel that allows banners, I would definitely advise you consider getting one made for you. It's another opportunity to communicate your brand. You can include a photo of you and/or your clients. It can show what you do or how you do it. Add your website URL and a strapline if you have one.

The digital honey trap

A word of warning about digital. It's easy to get bogged down, overwhelmed and distracted in this space, and that's certainly what happened to me. I made so many mistakes when I started out. I wasn't comfortable even talking to people until I had business cards and a complicated multipage website. I slowed myself down unnecessarily. I was constantly getting my website restructured and updating my multiple social media channels as I changed my branding over and over.

If I'd worked with a branding specialist upfront, I have no doubt my journey would have been much smoother. If I'd been more comfortable starting with something simple, I could have saved myself a lot of time, effort and money. I started off with one brand, then another and finally came right back round to the fact that I am the brand and anything else is unnecessarily complicated. It took me a long time and lots of unnecessary anguish to arrive at something I feel comfortable with. I hope you can avoid at least some of the mistakes I've made.

Our brain's primary function is to keep us safe. To achieve its objective, it creates obstacles and gives us reasons to slow down. Social media, branding and websites are all great examples of what many people starting their own businesses use as an excuse for why they're not quite ready yet.

Here are some common stalling tactics:

- I'm just waiting for some professional headshots/ images.

- I need to write some more website copy.

- Which social media handles should I use?

- I'm not sure which social media channels to pick.

- How often should I post? What should I say?

Many new business owners get caught up in the digital honey trap. It's important to be clear about your brand and your values upfront as they'll help guide you. But your offerings and message will likely evolve as you work with your first few clients, and so trying to nail everything down too early in the process, as I tried to do, will only cost you precious time, headspace and money.

It's understandable that you want to look professional, but it's important to understand that you don't have a business when you have a product. You have a business when you have a *client*. Your job is to find one client and then one more. And the truth is that your first few clients probably won't even look at your website or business card. The only thing they'll be impressed by is you, either because they already know, like and trust you directly, or have been referred by someone who does.

I'm hoping you're not feeling overwhelmed. Please keep it simple. We're in research mode for now. If you're worried about falling into the digital honey trap, it's time to move on.

OVER TO YOU: KEEP IT SIMPLE

Make some notes on the name you'll use and the information you'll have on your one-page website. Decide which social channel feels right for you and your potential clients.

CHAPTER 10

Offer – What Are You Selling?

'Don't push people to where you want to be.
Meet them where they are.'

— Meghan Keaney Anderson, Chief Marketing
Officer for The Wanderlust Group[20]

Now you've looked at your market, where your first few clients will come from and what you need digitally to get started, it's time to consider what you'll be selling.

In this chapter, we'll talk about your offering. How to construct it, how to price it and how to test it.

---

20 'Meet them where they are…', Executive-Women.me, 2020, https://
executive-women.me/meet-them-where-they-are

How to construct your offer

You may have a very clear idea of what you'll be offering, or it may be at more of a conceptual stage. 'If I could go back and tell myself two years ago,' Anish told me. 'I would have left with more than just a thought of what I wanted to do. I'd have had some sort of crystalised offer.'

A logical place to start when considering how to construct your offer may be your current employer. Do they charge their current clients by the hour or per project? Do they work on a time and materials basis or a fixed-price statement of work arrangement? Are you planning on offering a similar service, or will your point of difference be that you package things differently for your clients? If you currently work serving internal clients, this won't be so straightforward to calculate, but your current employer may still be a good place to begin.

Your potential clients have a problem, and they need a solution. People don't want a hammer or a nail. They want a picture on the wall. They care much less about *how* you solve their problem. What's important is the end result. What are you actually selling? What outcome do you achieve for your clients? Once you are clear about that, you can think about how that translates into a product or service.

Let's consider how to package up what you do in a way that will take your clients from where they are today to where they want to be. For any type of outcome or result, there will be three types of buyers:

- Those who want to figure it out themselves (Do It Yourself)

- Those who want help and support through the process (Done With You)

- Those who just want to pay for a solution and have someone else fix their problem for them (Done For You)

If you think about anything you've ever considered buying, you'll have put yourself into one of those three categories. The one you choose will be different for every single purchase, although you may have a natural tendency towards one category. Your choice will depend on factors like how you feel about the outcome you're looking at, how interested you are in the process, and how much time and money you have.

Let's look at each of these buyer categories in more detail, and I'll use myself and this book as an example. My potential client is you. You need assistance with how to transition from being an employee to running your own successful business serving multiple clients. I know how to do that, not only because I've done it myself, but because I've helped many others to do the same. But for you to be able to leverage the knowledge and experience I have, I need to package it for you.

Do It Yourself (DIY)

This is where you teach people how to do it themselves. It's a great solution because it's inexpensive for the client and you're empowering people by teaching them how to solve their own problems, which is positive.

Video training offers high value, especially if you also provide the audio to download, so your clients can listen to it while on the move. You can also include a workbook for them to work through, to give people a sense of making progress. We all like ticking things off a list! Private online community groups are an important part of offering your DIY clients value and allows them to meet and support others who are going through the same process as them. You'll find that they'll answer one another's questions and coach each other, so that the community becomes a highly valuable element of your service.

My offering to DIY clients is this book. It's low-cost, full of great value and it will help you through the process of transitioning from employee to business owner. However, it serves another purpose. It helps you get to know me, to understand the way I think and explain things, and it gives you a sense of what working with me might be like.

It may not be immediately obvious to you how you would create an offering for DIY clients, but if you put your mind to it, it's likely that you can. Is there part of your service that they could do themselves with your guidance? Are there questions you can provide answers to?

Done With You (DWY)

This is where you teach someone how to do something and you mentor them through actually doing it, either on a one-to-one basis, or in groups.

This option is more expensive because it involves your time, but it's a powerful way for your clients to learn and provides you with invaluable insights into what other problems they have that you might be able to solve. Try to avoid simply charging by the hour. Much better to package up your knowledge with training materials and also include one-to-one time if you're working with a group.

In my business, if you're a DWY client, you'll likely want to enquire about my programme where I take groups of people through the process outlined in this book. We work through each step together, you get to meet and collaborate with other people going through the exact same steps as you, facing the same doubts and fears as perhaps you are, and you get to ask me all the questions I haven't been able to answer in this book. For your business, a DWY offering may be consulting directly with your clients, advising them what they need to do.

Done For You (DFY)

For the third group, you offer to do the service for them. This is a premium offering. You need to think about what kind of services you want to sell here. Are you offering strategy and supervising the implementation or doing the work yourself? Do you need to hire project managers, developers, designers?

You may not have an offering for the DFY clients. In my case, I can't actually take you from being an employee to having a successful business. I can support you, but it's up to you to do the work. What I offer to my DFY clients is individual support and accountability in addition to my programme. In your case, you may do work for your clients.

The purpose of sharing this with you is to get you thinking about how you might be able to package the value you offer to your clients. They don't care about the time or the process. What they care about is the result they get at the end.

One other aspect to consider as you're looking at your offer is recurring revenue. What could you offer your clients that they could pay for every month, every quarter, or every year? Building up a steady stream of income allows you to plan.

Caroline has been running her brand and digital marketing business for thirteen years and in the last three or four has focused on retainer income. In addition to one-off projects like website builds or catalogue design, she also offers products including regular content creation and website enhancements that are paid for monthly. 'Having retainer products has helped me grow my team,' she told me. 'I can trial new products knowing that I have a foundation of revenue coming in.'

One last point about your offer. It's important to understand that people are creatures of emotion who buy what we want, not what we need.

As human beings, what we want is quite simple:

- To feel safe and secure

- To feel comfortable

- To be cared for and connected to others

- To be desired by others

- To be free to do what we want

- To grow and become more

- To serve others and give back

- To be surprised and excited

- To believe there is a higher purpose

- To feel that we matter

The challenge is to find a way to give your client both what they want *and* what they need. If you only give them what they want, it probably won't work and they'll blame you! Henry Ford is often, and likely inaccurately, quoted as saying, 'If I'd asked customers what they wanted, they would have told me "a faster horse"!'

You may feel the need to nail down your offering before you make any decisions or you might prefer to let it evolve over time, as I did. One lady told me that she had expected to focus on coaching but had actually found herself responding to work in the sustainability space. 'I haven't done any prospecting yet,' she said. 'Partly because I haven't known what to sell myself as. I feel like I need to let that emerge a bit, and not bucket myself.' Her plan is to give herself a few months to nail down her proposition. In my case it took longer than that.

What to charge

One of the biggest questions many people have is what to charge. Sophie provides financial services to small businesses and she told me it took her a few years to get right 'knowing what people would pay, what others were charging, what's too much and what's too little.'

In terms of pricing, your current employer is a great place to start, although you'll need to take into account any additional services or peace of mind they're able to offer clients that perhaps you can't (yet). On the other hand, any advantage they have may be offset by your ability to move more quickly, so don't be too quick to lower your prices.

You also need to look back at Chapter 7 (Earnings), where we crunched your numbers. How much do you need to be taking home after tax and all expenses?

It's very challenging to raise your prices with a client once you've started working with them. As far as possible, define specific packages of work so you can adjust your prices for future work if you want to. In most cases, price adjustments will be applied to new clients so think carefully about what you decide to charge.

Try not to charge for your time. Your client wants solutions, outcomes, so think about how you could price those rather than simply an hourly or daily rate. You could also consider having different price ranges depending on the size of client and complexity of the work.

Take a look at what the other players in your market are doing in terms of pricing. One interviewee found that 'there is no right answer to what you should charge for yourself.' They told me they did a survey of about ten people who did work they considered broadly comparable in terms of value. The results of their mini-poll were astonishing. They found that the highest amount that someone was charging was twenty times the lowest amount.

Ultimately, although you'll need to test your market, your decisions around pricing will come down to you deciding what you want to charge and then finding the people who match. To quote one of my interviewees: 'You are worth what you believe you're worth, and people will believe you're worth what you say you're worth.'

Testing

Ideally, you'd be able to test your new offering before you leave employment. Taking on your current employer as your first client can be a great way to test out your services in a lower-risk way. This may not be possible in your situation, but it's worth considering how and if you could before taking the plunge. Could you take on a paid client or two on the side before you leave? 'Ask your family or friends if you can trial something,' Anish suggests, 'in return for some open, honest feedback.'

When I left banking, it wasn't because I didn't enjoy the work. In fact, I loved running multiple programmes, being a 'right-hand woman' and managing large teams of great people. I wanted to be able to serve multiple clients at once but part-time engagements are rare in banking and I ended up leaving before I was able to test my services with any paying clients.

Caroline started to see signs of potential restructuring within her corporate employer and began preparing herself: 'I started doing a bit of design work for family and friends in my spare time, evenings and weekends. By the time the redundancy came, I had a portfolio to show potential clients and was ready to set up my own brand and digital marketing agency.'

Sophie's been working with small businesses as a part-time CFO for seven years. She told me that if it's possible, going down to four days a week in your paid employment to try out running your own business on your day off can be a really great way to do a trial run. 'Don't quit if you don't have a plan!' she said and, 'Do your research. Make sure there's a market for what you're offering.'

Even if you can't test your product or offering, you can test the selling of it. Talk to people, tell them what you're doing, ask them for their feedback and if they know anyone who might be interested. I know people who have offered their service for free. If you're trying something new, this is one way to try it out on a real client and get their feedback.

OVER TO YOU: SKETCH OUT YOUR PROPOSAL

Take some time to consider what product or service you'll start with and how you'll price it. Nothing is final but for now, let's sketch out a simple proposal. What are you selling? What problem does it solve? How will you deliver it and how much will you charge?

CHAPTER 11

Mindset – Getting Your Head In The Right Place

'A man cannot be comfortable without his own approval.'
— Mark Twain, American writer[21]

The decision of whether to leave employment is one of the biggest you're likely to make in your life. Deciding to go it alone requires mental toughness, a leap of faith and a shift in your mindset. In this chapter, we'll look at some of the things you'll need to get your head around to make this important decision.

Confidence and clarity

Working for yourself is a very different reality from working for someone else. The actual work may be

---

21 From 'What Is Man?', a short story published in 1906

similar, but nothing else is. It's personal. Clients are no longer being assigned to you, they are choosing to work with you. Even though you're likely to be drawing a salary from your new business, you'll raise invoices from your company and clients will pay them. It's a very different feeling.

Some find it liberating, others terrifying. Most people feel something between the two, at least for the first few months. You'll need to prepare yourself for an emotional rollercoaster and build up your resilience. For Nancy, the most challenging thing about running her own business is 'continually having to believe in yourself.' She has improved over time but still finds herself having a constant dialogue with herself: *You can do this and you're doing it, so stop talking nonsense!*

Confidence is key here, and it must come from inside. I can help you make the transition, but ultimately, you'll need to decide that you're good enough, that you can make it work. It comes down to backing yourself. The first sale you make is to yourself and that's where your confidence comes from.

One interviewee told me that the best thing about doing their own thing is that they're able to be excellent at their job. 'It's not anyone else acknowledging it. I'm being excellent at my job and I acknowledge that it's me.' They said that they tend to put themself down and find compliments hard to take. 'I'm working on my own, being excellent at what I do and being really proud of every single report that I write. And then when the clients come back to me, and it's all because of me, that's an amazing feeling.'

If you're leaving employment with negative feelings towards your work, it may take a bit of adjustment to be able to see yourself clearly. 'Now that I've been able to reflect a bit,' one interviewee told me, 'I'm really proud of what I've achieved and I'm excited to be proud of myself and everything I'm doing to make this work.'

One of the most important things you'll have to get your head around is learning to value yourself for something other than being busy. I advised you earlier to avoid charging for your time, and this is a big mindset shift for many. If you're a high achiever, you're probably used to being busy, and you may even think that being busy makes you valuable. To be honest, I've really struggled to learn this lesson. I love being busy. I love juggling. I love being efficient and organised. However, I've learned over the years that the real value I give my clients is being able to cut through all the noise, all the chaos, all the confusion, and help them see what's really there at the heart of the issue. If I'm busy and overwhelmed, my ability to do that effectively diminishes significantly.

Like mine, your clients will come to you because they want a solution. And the truth is that they don't care if it takes you two seconds or two days to figure it out for them or with them. They don't care if your process happens in the shower or while you're walking your dog. What they care about is that you can fix their problem, take their pain away, show them a better way.

During the tough days, which will inevitably come, your knowledge that what you do is valuable will carry you through. Your one-page website is a great place to come back to. Make sure it tells everyone, including the bit of you that still doubts this decision, exactly what you do and for whom. Make sure it clearly states what problem you solve and what makes you uniquely special. This is what you need to hold on to as you decide whether to make this transition. Be ready for the fact that how you see yourself and what you offer may change over time.

Backing yourself means recognising that you have options. Katy told me that even if she couldn't make this work, the process of making the decision had opened her eyes to all the opportunities available to her. 'What's the worst that can happen?' she asked herself. 'Now that I'm backing myself, my confidence and trust that I can make it work is building.'

Beware of overconfidence

On the other end of the spectrum from doubting yourself is arrogance. As a confident person, being arrogant is a fear I choose to carry with me. I ask myself regularly if I'm being arrogant or overconfident. It's something I ask my coach to watch out for. His view is that my compassion and willingness to learn keep me on the right side of the line, but early in my entrepreneurial life, it definitely tripped me up.

My story: Have you ever started something thinking it'd be easy?

My first book started in the summer of 2017, when I quickly rattled off 40,000 words. I was overconfident and sure I'd be done by Christmas. I was good at writing essays at school and university. It was just a longer version – how hard could it be?

The problem was I wasn't clear on what I was saying, who I was saying it to, or what problem I was trying to solve. I ignored most of the advice given to me by my publisher, and I really paid the price. I also completely underestimated the emotional challenge. Was it good enough? Would anyone read it? How could I put something out there that was so permanent with my name on?

Luckily, I had amazing beta readers who gave me honest and robust feedback, and several great supporters pushing and encouraging me, but I still spent many months wrestling with the content and structure while battling procrastination and self-doubt. Finally, two years after I started, *The REAL Entrepreneur* was published on 24 June 2019.

I was absolutely terrified until the Amazon reviews started appearing:

> *I was struck by how relevant this book was to me as a small business owner.*
>
> *In a time when I have sometimes doubted myself and why I have become a kind of accidental entrepreneur, I sometimes need to read a book that reaffirms why I did it, and what I need to take ME to the next level – this is that book!*
>
> *Can't recommend it enough.*
>
> *Thank you for writing this book!*

I felt so relieved that people were not only responding positively but finding value in my work. We ran a promotion in the autumn and the book went to the top of the rankings on Amazon, beating Elon Musk and Simon Sinek in the competitive Small Business and Entrepreneurship category. What a completely surreal experience! I still receive at least one message every week telling me how much my book helped the reader and their business, which makes all the stress and the doubt worthwhile.

I often think back to that time and try hard to learn the lessons. Working for yourself is about learning, and that's often uncomfortable. We all make mistakes and that's also part of the process. Finding that sweet spot of self-confidence, a perfect balance between self-doubt and arrogance, is a lifelong journey for many, including me.

This second book has been a completely different experience. I was very clear from the start who exactly I was writing for and what I wanted to say. I hope that what you're taking from it is that you deserve to be confident in who you are and what you do.

Who else will this impact?

So far, we've talked a lot about you. This is your life and your decision. But depending on your circumstances, your decision will also impact those around you.

It can be tough deciding to leave a well-paid and secure job if your partner is not supportive. You risk putting a huge strain on your relationship if you cannot get their buy-in. Building a business is hard and takes a lot of energy, so it's important to ensure you have good support around you. 'I've put Martina through hell so many times,' Francis told me. 'If it wasn't for her unbelievable support, I would never be where I am today. I needed that grounding, knowing everything was OK at home with the kids. Without that I wouldn't have been able to focus my energy on building the business.'

Andy described how supportive his wife was of his decision. 'Mildly crazy of her considering we had two young children at the time, and I was the sole source of income.' She knew he had a clear plan and timeline in which to make it work and she gave him her full support.

Anish also talked about looking at your support network, especially if you're married, with a partner or have children. 'Look at how much time you'll have available to develop this,' he advised.

You can make this work without the support of your loved ones, but it will be much easier and you'll be much more likely to succeed if you have their backing. 'You don't need that battle to fight,' Anish told me.

OVER TO YOU: WHAT'S IMPORTANT TO YOU?

Before moving on, please write down what makes you valuable and what gives you confidence. Capture the words that you'll say to yourself about why you want this, about why it's important to you. Decide who this decision will impact and who you want to consult.

CHAPTER 12

Decision Time

'When you come to a fork in the road, take it.'
— Yogi Berra, baseball player and manager[22]

We've come to the end of the FREEDOM Formula, and I hope that you now have much more clarity about the decision you face.

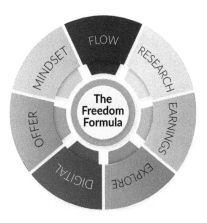

---

22   Y Berra, *The Yogi Book* (Workman Publishing, 1998)

We've looked at **flow** and doing things your way. We've talked about what **research** would be advantageous to do. In the **earnings** chapter, you crunched your numbers and calculated your runway and burn rate, and in the **explore** chapter, we got you talking to your network and thinking about who your first clients will be. We looked at the **digital** world and what you'll need to get started and we considered how to structure and price your **offer**. Finally, we discussed your **mindset** and where you'll need to get your head to make this transition.

At the start of Part Two, I told you we were gathering information and reviewing our options. Remember I advised you to reassure your brain by telling it you hadn't decided yet? That was true then, but now it's decision time.

As Austin put it during our interview: 'While "prior planning and preparation prevents poor performance", to paraphrase the British army adage, there's also a need for balance by channelling Elvis Presley: more action and less conversation.'

Your brain will always want more information, more data. It will always want to stall in its efforts to keep your safe. Justin's advice is to know yourself first, so you are better placed to make informed decisions when taking calculated risks: 'Self-reflection is vital, but action is required. Understand the risks but don't let them put you off,' he told me. 'Understand why you're doing it.' He shared with me how the words of a tattoo he'd seen on the arm of a barmaid ten years ago – *My freedom rests on my willingness to lose everything* – resonated with him as the credo required for undertaking the entrepreneur's journey. We spoke about the importance of understanding the implications of your decisions on the important relationships in your life. 'Thinking about the broader context of your decisions is key.'

I remember one of my mentors talking about that moment at the end of your life where you meet the version of yourself that you could have been. The idea sent a chill down my spine and still does. All the possibilities and potential we have inside us, waiting and wanting to be fulfilled. Like me, Francis talks about regretting the things you don't do rather than those you do. Despite losing his first business and facing some serious challenges, he still advises people considering this move: 'Just go for it! The sooner you start, the better. Fail fast. It'll give you amazing satisfaction every day. It's really tough but so rewarding. I wake up every morning saying thank you, thank you, thank you.'

Andy's advice is, 'Jump on in. The water's lovely, but look out for sharks and whirlpools.'

The truth is, you won't know how you're going to feel until you've made the decision. Katy described a process of 'surrendering to the decision and things falling into place as your confidence grows.'

Try this tool to help you move forward.

Tool – A decision meditation

Give yourself some time and space to consider:

- How will I feel in five years' time if I stay in employment?

- How will I feel in five years' time if I start my own thing?

- What would the me in five years' time tell me?

- What's the worst thing that could happen?

- What's the best thing that could happen?

Sit with these questions and see what comes up. What are your hopes and fears?

Nancy told me about her process. 'The thing that frightens you most, that you're really putting off doing, do it! Because that will unlock everything. Every time I've done that, it's never been anywhere near as bad as I thought it was going to be. And most of the time it's been a really good thing to do and has actually opened another door for me.' Her advice is just to go for it. 'Take just one step,' she told me, 'because as soon as you do, then you're doing it, you're moving.'

You've done the work, you've gathered the information you need and you're ready. We've reached the moment for you to consider your options and decide what you want to do. If, after looking at everything, you decide to stay in employment, then I wish you good fortune and the best of luck in your choice. If, however, you decide that you're ready to take the plunge, then let's move on to Part Three.

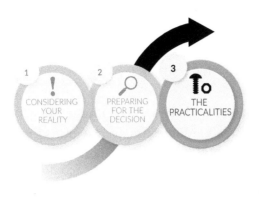

PART THREE

THE PRACTICALITIES

Now the decision's been made, how do you feel? Take a moment to enjoy the clarity you have. You've decided to make a big change in your life and that deserves some recognition. If you haven't done so already, tell yourself that you're proud that you're taking this step (even if you're also a bit scared!).

Congratulations and welcome to the wonderful world of the entrepreneur. It will be a rollercoaster ride for sure, but remember that it's a marathon rather than a sprint. You don't need to know it all and you definitely don't have to do it all. Although you may well start out as Andy did – 'I didn't know who I was going to bring in or when, so I worked off the assumption that

I needed to know everything' – in time, you will build up resources that you can leverage.

This decision is likely to have a huge impact on your life, but don't underestimate the transition period. 'It's incredibly clear to me,' one lady told me, 'that you can't just step out of corporate life. You have to recalibrate everything about the way you live your life. The value you place on a good night's sleep or on taking the decision to not work seventy hours a week.'

Ideally, you want to give yourself some time to adjust to the new reality. If you can factor in some adjustment time between employment and starting work with your new clients, so much the better. 'I think it took me a month or so before I got my head around the idea of not getting up at 5am,' one interviewee told me. 'It feels like a relief, it feels like freedom, but it's also a grieving process.' For Katy, handing in her notice at work brought a big change in how she felt about herself. 'I've really been seeing myself as stand-alone. I'm not seeking validation anymore. It's given me the confidence that I can make this work.'

Be kind to yourself. However prepared you feel, it might still take time to adjust. 'If you're leaving corporate life going, "I know exactly what I'm doing, I've got my business plan, I'm off", then fine,' one interviewee told me. 'But if you need some time to transition, then give yourself the space you need.' Until you take the step, you don't know. So, on a practical level, give yourself the bridge or the space. But you're going on an emotional journey and you deserve the space to do that too. Structure things to give yourself that space.

It can feel like a huge change to leave the security of corporate life and embrace the life of an entrepreneur. It's one your brain may take a while to adjust to, so you'll need to be patient with yourself. Justin the psychotherapist believes life is about learning and taking risks. 'There's no failure, only feedback,' he told me. 'But our bodies and unconscious minds don't necessarily agree!' Give yourself the opportunity to process the change in your own way.

Some things you just won't be able to see or understand until you're there. One interviewee's experience was of 'a big wide world out there just waiting for you, but you're not going to see it until you step out into it.' They're now starting to realise that they'd underestimated the scope of possibilities. 'I'm on my own boat now, rather than a big corporate cruise ship, but I've got decisions to make about where I'm going to float my little boat. Until I was free of seventy hours a week, these things couldn't really percolate in my head.'

First things first. To avoid overwhelm, we need to make a plan.

It doesn't need to be complicated. It will include a list of things you want and need to do. It will also contain a timeline, which you can map to your calendar and use to set yourself goals.

Your plan will serve two purposes. First, it will help you figure out what you need to do and enable you to track your progress. Second, it will help you keep any negative emotions in check, that voice in your head that's sure to question your decision every now and then, those moments when it feels as if the universe is testing you. When you feel doubt – and you will – having a plan will enable you to reassure the voices of fear and anxiety. You will be able to show yourself that you have a plan that you're working through. If you notice yourself getting distracted or using excuses to second-guess yourself, you can use your plan to stay focused and ignore your questions and uncertainties. When in doubt, get your head down and stick to the plan.

Ironically, the things people worry about beforehand don't always turn to be the ones they find challenging. Caroline thought it would be really hard to find customers. 'The customers came. That was the easy part. It was actually running the business that was really hard. I didn't have a clue.' Andy spent his energy and focus on winning his first client. 'I remember coming out of winning my first deal, thinking, *How am I going to deliver this?* and that led to my first hire!' He described focusing on the fundamentals at the start: 'How do I make this a legal entity, how do I do accounting, how do I find business and how do I manage my contacts?'

Nancy told me about her initial feelings. 'It seems like this massive thing and it's all so overwhelming.' Her advice is to break everything down into steps and take them one at a time. 'As long as you're always taking a step forward, you're doing it. The paralysis of not doing it and wanting to is awful.'

At the beginning of every plan there needs to be a goal. Our primary goal is to establish you as a business owner with a steady stream of income and multiple clients. Do you have any specific goals that you want to add? Make sure you capture them.

- How many clients?

- How much time working? How much time off?

- How long to reach particular income milestones?

- New markets and products?

- New team members?

Just as important as your goals is your *why*. What are your reasons for wanting to make this transition? Why are you leaving, and what's important to you as you look forward? One lady told me that although financial success is part of what she wants to achieve, 'It's not all about the thrill of the chase and the size of the prize.' For her, it's about finding 'meaning in the work' she's doing.

In Part One of this book, we considered the pros and cons of making the transition. We looked at what you wanted and why. When times are tough or you hit a hurdle, it's important to have something to hang on to. Make sure your reasons are clear. They will sustain you through moments of doubt or difficulty.

In Part Two of this book, we looked at the various dimensions of the decision you've made. Now it's time to turn these into reality. In Part Three, we'll look at the practicalities of running a business and some business model options to consider as you grow. As we walk through this, make notes and add to your plan. Have a place where you capture things you want to do but not right away. Prioritise the things that will move you forward now.

CHAPTER 13

Business Model Options

'Write your principles in pen and your business model in pencil.'
— Unknown

Before we get to the practicalities, there's something you'll need to be keeping in the back of your mind. It's not necessarily something you'll need to spend a lot of time on right at the start of your business journey, but I want to give it to you now to file away for future consideration.

You may not think of yourself as a business owner just yet. Tamara describes herself as a freelancer and Nancy said it took her four months before she started to think of herself as a businesswoman or an entrepreneur. 'I've decided that I do want this to be a business,' she told me. 'I don't just want this to be me, which is quite a change from what I thought at the start.' Regardless of how you start out thinking about yourself, at some point in the not-too-distant future, your thoughts will probably turn from how to set up and run your business to how to grow it. That's when knowing what your options are in terms of a business model will be helpful.

The choice you make will impact what type of business you end up building. There's no right or wrong answer. As always, you've got to pick what's right for you.

One interviewee told me that three months in, they're asking themselves bigger questions than they did at the start. 'Do I want to collaborate with others and if so, what form does that take? Do I want to co-own a venture with somebody? Do I want to be part of a network that works collaboratively, but we're all independent? Do I actually want to work towards employment in a new way? Am I actually using this freedom to totally define who I am, but actually I may end up in employment again out of choice?' They said they want to create something that enables them to do work they can be proud of and that they could show their children. 'The fact that I haven't worked out exactly what it is yet is beside the point!'

It all comes down to what you want at a fundamental level. How ambitious are you? How important is independence to you? How much do you want to grow? What does work–life balance mean to you?

Didrik advises asking yourself some searching questions, such as, 'Why am I doing this?' and 'How far will I go to achieve it?'

Let's look at some options for your business model.

Solopreneur

One of the first business model decisions you're likely to make is whether you want or are able to handle all the client-facing aspects of your business yourself.

The advantage of doing so is that you have more control over when and where you work. The disadvantage is that you're limited by your time and you have no backup. One of the ways of mitigating this is by offering group programmes, online courses and other offerings that better leverage your time.

In reality, few business owners are truly alone in their business. I always encourage my clients to build a team around them to handle all the pieces they either don't want to do or others could do better, as well as to be always thinking about where they could put their time and energy to better use.

This is the model I've chosen. I still work one-to-one with some clients, but the majority of my time is spent running workshops and programmes that combine group work with one-to-one sessions. I also run an online community for business owners, which allows me to speak with many people at once. I am supported by a virtual assistant, graphic designer, videographer, accountant, and several others.

Consultancy

Building a consultancy involves you not being the only client-facing person in your business. You hire others who have similar or complementary skills and experience to you. You bring them in to do the pieces you can't or don't want to, or to assist or replace you. Perhaps you could kick off a piece of work and then hand it over to a member of your team, or you may choose to be the person winning the work and have a team who delivers.

The advantages of the consultancy model are that you can serve more clients and the business isn't entirely dependent on you. The downside is that you have a 'machine' to feed – people who need work, which someone has to find. The other disadvantage, especially if you're the one selling, is that the client may wish to buy you and your expertise. They may build trust with you and want you to be the only person who delivers them the service they've bought. If not handled properly, this can lead to you becoming a bottleneck in your business.

There are also many successful hybrid models. One is where the founder does some of the client delivery work but also finds work for others. In Sophie's case, she recruits other CFOs on a contract basis and places them with companies who need their services. She told me that she likes this model as she can balance and flex it, taking on more of the work herself or focusing more on the recruitment side depending on her needs. She is also able to make very clear to the client upfront that she is finding the right 'fit' for them, avoiding the bottleneck problem I mentioned above.

Nancy is planning to have a part of her business that's scalable. 'We're the contract administrators for the data centre sector,' she told me. She will still offer her own services at a premium, but she describes having part of her business as the 'bread and butter' where she can get other people in and get some traction in the market.

Partnership

You may consider setting up your business with one or more other people from the start. Being in a partnership definitely has its advantages. Someone to bounce ideas off, to make decisions with and to share the work. The biggest advantage is the ability to work with someone who complements you in terms of skills and approach, someone who loves doing the things that drain your energy. Each advantage has its flipside, and it will be up to you to decide if being in partnership is worth losing some of your autonomy and freedom.

During our interview, Didrik spoke about the importance of carefully considering who you choose to partner with. 'Don't be naïve,' he told me. 'This is as big as getting married or having kids.' We also talked about the difference between partnership and employment and the importance of business partners being on the same page. 'Being an entrepreneur is not a job, it's a life.' When I asked him if he thought he'd jumped in too quickly, he told me that in hindsight, a more in-depth analysis of the product and the market wouldn't have changed his decision. However, he also said, 'Awareness of the challenges of working with business partners who have different vision and values might have made me spend a bit more time evaluating different options.'

When considering starting a business partnership, it's vital to have an open and honest conversation about what you want and why. Partnerships can break down for many reasons. Often, they do so because expectations haven't been clearly stated from the start or because the partners realise that they don't want the same thing from the business. It's easy to muddle through when times are good. When you hit a rough patch, being on the same page about what you're doing and why it's important, can be the difference between staying together and drifting apart.

Here are some items to discuss, agree and put down in writing:

- What are you trying to achieve with the business? What are your aspirations?

- Do you want to exit? If so, what is your timeframe?

- What kind of business are you building? A lifestyle business to keep you and your families comfortable or are you chasing world domination?

- Who will be responsible for what? How will the effort be split?

- What is the time commitment from each of the parties?

- What happens if one of you gets ill or dies?

- What happens if one of you falls pregnant or has a change in family circumstances?

- What happens if one of you changes their mind about time commitment or job role?

- What happens if one of you decides you want to leave earlier than planned?

- What happens if you don't agree?

A good partnership is founded on shared values, outcomes and timelines. People change and so do their priorities, expectations and goals, which is why it's so important to get clear about what happens when they do upfront.

It's so much easier to have this conversation at the start, when things are harmonious, and you're excited by the prospect of working together. After months or years of hard work, when things get tough and people discover that they want different things, or their memory of conversations becomes tainted by experience, the best of friends can end up falling out and never speaking to each other again. The passing of time and the stress of running a business can change your memory or perception of things.

Even if you think you agree today, get it onto a piece of paper, just to be sure that you're (literally) on the same page. Something as simple as a memorandum of understanding can do wonders for clarifying what was agreed in a situation where both parties are convinced that their memory is correct.

If you're considering going into business with someone you don't know well, it can take time for trust to build. Clarity is key to ensure you stay on the same page and your expectations are aligned. Because of the traumatic experience of losing his first business to unscrupulous partners, Francis was much more cautious when setting up Westtek. He first met his business partner when he was pitching a deal and Graham was the IT Director giving him a really hard time. He didn't win that deal, but they did end up working together. 'We built up trust over time to the point where I was comfortable getting to a 49/51% split. But I had to retain control because of what happened to me before.' Three years ago, they started a sister company together to focus on cybersecurity and Francis described 'putting the demons to rest' by sharing the equity equally.

Training others

Another option is to train others to do what you do. Instead of serving clients directly, you train people on how to do so. If you're a Facebook Ads specialist, instead of running ad campaigns for clients, you could train people who want to learn more about advertising on Facebook so they can serve their own clients better.

The advantage of this is that it's scalable: you can train groups and even create online courses. The disadvantage is that you no longer deal directly with clients. You're no longer doing the work, instead you are training others to do it. This model can of course be combined with the others I've outlined above, but be careful not to stretch yourself too thin. Focus is key!

It's important to take time to really think about what will work for you. 'What is this for me?' one lady is asking herself, 'Is this a decision to have a better work– life balance, or is it about deciding my own direction and choosing work that's meaningful to me?' It could be both, of course, but they are very different decisions with very different implications. She's figuring out the 'shape and scale' of her ambition. 'What is the impact I want to have on the world?' Being married to a successful and very ambitious entrepreneur, she's also working hard not to let his journey and experience 'inform the decisions I make or pressure me to play on a stage that big.' She's focused on making her own conscious decisions about what's right for her.

There are no right or wrong answers here. Whichever model you choose, it's all about building something that works for you.

OVER TO YOU: DECIDE ON YOUR STARTING MODEL

You've made a decision and considered your options. How do you want to proceed? What model are you starting with and what are you driving towards? It's OK not to be sure. Go with what feels right and know that you can always change your mind.

CHAPTER 14

Taking The Plunge

'Take the first step in faith. You don't have to see the whole staircase, just take the first step.'
— Martin Luther King, American minister and activist[23]

Not only do you have a decision, but you know what your options are and may even have an idea of what you're building towards. It's time to take the plunge!

Although we've answered quite a few of your questions, I'm sure there are more surfacing every day.

- When do you give notice at work?

- When do you form your company?

- When do you tell people?

---

23 BA Reynolds, *And Still We Rise: Interviews with 50 Black role models* (USA Today Books, 1988)

There are no right or wrong answers. There are elements of setting up you can do while still employed, but there are also plenty of advantages to drawing a line and making your intentions clear.

In my experience, until you give your notice in at work, many aspects of this decision won't feel real. As soon as you take the plunge, things will feel different. Be prepared for an emotional rollercoaster those first few days and weeks. Remind yourself of why you made your decision and what's important to you. Once you're on the other side, it will be easier to flesh out your plan.

Strictly speaking, you don't need to form your company until you're ready to raise your first invoice, but this may also be different depending on where you are in the world. Get advice from your accountant, who will be able to guide you on appropriate timelines. In this chapter, we'll look at some of your immediate challenges and areas of focus.

Communication

Your network is likely to continue to be an important source of support as you grow your business. All those people you've connected with over the years may generate plenty of referrals, introductions and collaborations.

The decision on how and when to communicate your decision is an individual one. You'll need to think about what feels appropriate and how you want to go about it.

Nancy waited a few months before updating her LinkedIn profile, whereas Katy wanted to 'own the message from day one' rather than anybody else communicating about how or why she was leaving. I waited until I felt I had everything lined up before going public, but you may feel ready to do it straight away. Trust your instincts.

Budget

Are you someone who tells themselves they're not good with numbers? Too many business owners leave everything to their accountants, which can be a mistake. Your accountant's job is to ensure that you're compliant with the law, relevant regulations and the tax authorities. They'll certainly advise you and they're likely to be an invaluable source of information, but ultimately, you're the one running your business. The bottom line is, you need to know your numbers so that you can make decisions.

The reason many businesses fail is not because they don't have income, but because their owners aren't on top of their numbers. Let's make sure that doesn't happen to you. In Chapter 7 (Earnings), we looked at your numbers, so you already have a sense of this, but now we need to make a budget. It doesn't need to be anything complicated, but it's a vital part of your plan and how you run your business.

If you haven't already done so, map out your planned business earnings across time. When are you going to sign each client and how long will you work with them? When will you invoice them and when will they pay? Map out your costs in the same way so you can see how your cash flow looks. Don't forget to include what you need to take out each month.

Talking of cash flow, we also need a simple spread-sheet that maps out in detail what you expect to come in and out of your business bank account over the next three months and when. Have a running total so you can see the balance as you go. Add in when you expect to receive any money from clients, and when you expect to have to pay any costs.

This is not about accounting principles but about managing your cash. I would highly recommend that you maintain a similar document for your personal finances.

There are three key numbers that every business owner needs to know:

- What do you need personally?

- What are your business costs?

- And therefore, what revenue do you need?

As we discussed in Chapter 7 (Earnings), you also need to keep an eye on your runway. How long will your business and personal cash last?

One of the most important challenges for small businesses is to keep a handle on cost and ensure they're not spending money on things they don't need. I certainly made this mistake in the first year or so of my business, paying subscriptions for software I didn't end up needing and training courses I subsequently decided weren't relevant to my business. Francis told me about the importance he places on keeping a handle on costs, especially after the trauma of losing his first business. 'One year I spent £87,000 on different systems, thinking it would really improve the business. It was madness! Now we outsource what we can, and everything is on a monthly basis. It gives me much better control over the ups and downs in expenditure.'

I asked at the beginning of this section if you're someone who tells themselves they're not good with numbers. If that's you, then I want to challenge the narrative you're telling yourself. What you probably mean is that you don't like thinking about numbers or dealing with spreadsheets, which is, of course, totally fine. I'm not actually saying you need to do the crunching, but you do need to be responsible for it. Get your accountant to provide you with the numbers but take responsibility for asking questions and understanding what you're being shown. Nancy describes turning what was a barrier for her into a positive: 'Taking control of my finances and knowing what I can and can't do is a revelation.'

One important point about managing your numbers – what you choose to pay yourself is not the same as the profit your business makes. Your salary is a business expense. The money that's left over after you've paid all your expenses, including your own salary, can be used to invest in further training, acquiring new clients, putting in systems and hiring additional people. Seeing your business as a separate entity is something that may take time to adjust to.

It's easy to get carried away in your first year and forget that the tax authorities will want their slice of your profits. One way to be sure you'll have enough money to pay your tax bill is to open a separate business bank account for tax and transfer in a percentage of every payment you receive. Your accountant will be able to help you calculate the correct amount, but having a separate account is a good way to separate out the tax money from the start.

Getting help

Working for yourself can get lonely, so it's important to have people around you who lift you up. We've already talked about the importance of your network, whether it's friends and family, other business owners, or people you can collaborate with. But there's also the people who can do work for you and support your business. Austin talked about having capable people around, whether partners or service providers. 'You've got to know who you can rely on,' he told me.

If you've come from a large corporate, you'll be used to being able to take a great many things for granted. 'You don't worry about the sales or the finances.' Caroline told me, 'You only know your area, how to do your job.' She described hiring a coach to cover the basics of running a business as 'the best thing I ever did.'

One interviewee told me that they needed to work through what was going on in their head with a coach before they were ready to move forward. 'Get help to establish what it is that you're after, and then structure a plan to make it real.' That's one of the reasons why I wrote this book, to help people along the journey. It's easy to feel alone, but others have been where you are, struggled with similar challenges and found a way through. Like me, Didrik recommends connecting with other people who are on a similar journey to gain inspiration and support but also to avoid going mad!

You cannot do everything and nor should you. Remember one of the questions from Chapter 5

(Flow): 'Which aspects of what your clients will want from you are you going to enjoy, and which tasks will be more of a chore?'

Justin describes the admin of running a business as 'the antithesis of creativity.' Like many business owners, the admin is the very opposite of the things he enjoys, that motivate him and that he's good at. 'It's soul destroying,' he told me. 'It's mind-numbingly boring and dull and I hate it!' Many people hate admin. If that's you, then get yourself a virtual assistant. If you're not very creative, how about a designer? Just because you can do something, doesn't mean you should!

From the outset, think about building a team. Remember, you don't need to employ people if you don't want to. There are plenty of very capable self-employed contractors who can do everything from social media to fixing your tech issues, designing your brochure to answering your emails. You remain responsible of course, it's still your business, but start as you mean to go on. Focus your energy, time and headspace on those things that you're good at, that light you up and put you in flow.

There are certainly advantages to having employees, though. You may feel more secure when they're 'your people'. Caroline used to employ contractors to work in her marketing agency but told me that bringing everybody in-house gave her the confidence to raise her prices. Without a team, you've got a finite number of hours and your scaling options are more limited.

Your accountant needs to be a key member of your team from the start. You want to find someone you can trust to tell you what you need to know. Francis told me about the importance he places on having an accountant who 'keep us on our toes' as he's running his IT services company. 'We now have management accounts every single month with very clear outcomes and goals, whereas my previous accountant used to come round once a year. By the time I realised I had a problem, it was far too late.' He told me that unless your accountant is 'keeping you accountable, you're wasting your time. Get a new one!'

Nancy had tried being a contractor before and one of the things that really put her off setting up her own business was managing and figuring out all the numbers. I told her that often when we get stuck on things, a better question than *how* is *who?* She found an accountant who could produce the numbers she needed and explain them to her in a way that makes sense to her. What had previously seemed like a huge blocker quickly disappeared as an issue.

Of course, having a team and dealing with people, whether employees or outsourced contractors, means managing people – and that's definitely a skill. 'Find out what you can do better than others,' Andy told me. 'Do more of it and delegate what you aren't so good at quickly. But understand what you're delegating. Don't just hand it off and hope.'

Managing people

Managing people is all about being clear – setting clear expectations and asking questions rather than thinking you need to have all the answers. It's about being straightforward with people and helping them do the best job they can. Not in your way but in theirs. Yes, you set the standard, you get to define what 'good' looks like and you dictate the desired outcome. But getting the best from your people means learning to accept that there's more than one way to get from A to B.

My story: 'Remember you're not there to make friends, Lisa. You're there to do a job!'

When I first started working, I used to think you had to know what everyone was doing to be a good manager. At the very least, I decided that to progress up the ladder, I needed to know more than the people around me. I also used to believe that nobody could or would do things as well as me. I found it hard to trust anyone else to do things in my way or to my standards. I was working in a big corporate company, climbing up the ranks and taking on more and more responsibility. I thought the only way was to work harder and harder. I put my health and family life at risk.

What changed for me was that back in 2002, I got the opportunity for a fantastic new role in India. It involved managing a large team in an area of the business I knew nothing about. I remember when I first saw the announcement of my new role. I was so excited! I forwarded it on to my mentor at the time. He'd been such a great support to me and I knew he'd be delighted. His reply took me by surprise: 'Remember you're not there to make friends, Lisa. You're there to do a job!'

When I read his words, I felt like I had ice running down the back of my neck. What did he mean? His words sounded cold and unfeeling and brought on an avalanche of fear. *'What will they think of me? What do I know about the Indian market or these products? What value can I really add to them if I don't understand what they're doing?'*

I remember the moment I met the first member of my new team. We were in the Delhi city office and someone had just called out, 'The boss lady is here!' Everyone on the whole floor was looking at me. It was something I had to get used to pretty quickly as it happened everywhere I went, but that first time still sticks in my head.

I also remember the first time I got the team together as they were based all over India. We were all just chatting informally, getting to know one another before I officially kicked off the meeting, and one man came up to me to introduce himself. He proudly told me he hadn't taken a day's holiday in five years. 'Well, I will be taking every single one of my vacation days and I expect you all to do the same!' Maybe I spoke a little too forcefully or maybe they were all kind of listening anyway while pretending they weren't, but everyone stopped talking and turned to look at me. I think we all knew in that moment that our lives were never going to be the same.

I felt overwhelmed by the new culture. Everything was *so* different from what I was used to, but I focused on what my mentor had told me: just getting the job done. I worked on giving my team a clear structure and ways of operating. I ensured they knew what was expected of them. And I focused on asking questions and listening to what they said. I asked them what they enjoyed about their roles and what they struggled with.

I learned that the complete opposite of what I'd believed turned out to be true. What my team needed from me was not knowledge about their market or products, but guidance, coaching and structure. They needed to know where they stood with me and they needed to know that I had their back. I would ask them what obstacles they faced and then help them overcome them. I didn't need to understand all the details of what they were doing every day. When they brought a problem to me, I would ask them about it. Clarity turned out to be the most valuable aspect of being a manager.

Every time a challenging situation arose, and they certainly did, I would send a silent 'thank you' to my mentor back in Xerox HQ. I had to fire a couple of people, I had to deal with allegations of corruption and worse. It was certainly an interesting and educational experience. And through it all, I held on to those wise words – probably the best piece of management advice I've ever received.

One of the challenges but also opportunities that comes from today's connected world is the ability to work with people remotely. Austin told me that his team has always worked remotely as they serve clients around the world, providing strategic research, due diligence and corporate communications. He told me that working remotely 'requires discipline but can be liberating if mastered appropriately.' I definitely agree. The ability to work from wherever I am in the world, connecting with my clients and team as I go, is a key driver for me.

Working with other people and building a team is one of the best aspects of running a business for many people. Most successful entrepreneurs will tell you about the importance of surrounding yourself with great people. 'Having a business partner you can trust and working with a team that just "gets" you is priceless,' Francis told me. 'Working together every day to achieve a common objective. For me, that's the best part of running my own business.'

Juggling activities

One of the things you may notice as you make the transition is how your relationship with time changes. The realisation that you have total control over your diary can be a revelation. 'I remember looking at this broad expanse of diary,' Andy told me, 'and thinking – *what shall I fill that with?*' The truth is that you still have to work, and potentially harder than you ever did when you were employed. As Anish put it, 'You just get to choose which twelve hours you work.'

Although there's an element of juggling conflicting tasks and priorities in any job, when you run your own business, the number of different things you need to think about and keep a track of can be daunting. One of my interviewees told me about the challenges of being disciplined. 'I'm very drawn in different directions by my curiosity.' Many business owners love the strategic thinking and setting things up but struggle with the rigour of maintaining structure.

Discipline is also something that concerns Tamara. During our interview, she confessed that she's worried about the slippery slope. 'Maybe I'll take the morning off and then the next one. And suddenly I'm watching television all day in my pyjamas and not earning anything!' She told me that she worries that she'll enjoy the freedom too much. She acknowledged that it's unlikely and that she's much more likely to 'burn myself out because I'm so passionate about it and I won't know when to stop.'

As business owners, it's very common to feel overwhelmed by all the decisions we need to make and options we have to choose from. We often find ourselves working harder and harder with no real plan of how to change things. We tell ourselves that we're almost there, that things will get less busy soon, without really knowing how we'll achieve that!

It's important to have a system for keeping your head clear. One that helps you manage your time and priorities. One that enables you to focus on what's important so you can make good decisions for your business. One that doesn't rely on your memory.

We've talked a lot about our brains already and they have a crucial role to play here too. Every time we commit to doing anything, our brains open what's called a 'loop'. The problem is that they can't tell the difference between something urgent that needs to be done today and something we might get round to someday, one day. They also can't distinguish between something small, like changing a light bulb, and something huge, like selling a business.

This means that our heads get cluttered with 'stuff' we need to remember and our brains (whose primary function is to keep us safe) keep trying to be helpful and remind us of everything we've 'committed' to doing. That's why you may find yourself awake at night thinking about a book someone mentioned to you or worrying that you might forget a call you're planning to make.

The only way to avoid overwhelm and clear your head is to have some sort of a system. It doesn't matter whether it's pen and paper or the latest tech, it must be something that works for you. Whatever system you use, it must convince your brain that you have a way of remembering and keeping on top of all your commitments, however large or small. This is the only way to close all those open loops in your head. That's because unless your brain trusts you've got a system that works, it will keep on trying to remember everything and it will keep reminding you.

Whatever system you use needs to work for you. What works for me may not work for you. Some people like structure, others prefer something more fluid. Some choose to use pieces of paper, maybe several different notebooks, and others want everything together in an online system.

When I work with my clients on getting organised, I use another formula – the FOCUS Formula. It's adaptable to you and your needs and is customisable to each individual.

Tool – The FOCUS Formula

This formula has five steps. You'll probably find that you're doing some or all of these, but to keep your head clear, you need to be doing each of the five consistently.

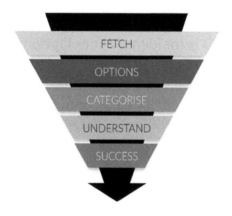

Step One: F is for Fetch everything

Every time you have a thought about maybe, possibly, one day, should, could, would, might do something, a loop opens in your brain.

As your brain has no sense of time, you must fetch or capture everything. It really doesn't matter if you use a piece of paper, an app on your phone, multiple notebooks or a spreadsheet. What's vitally important is that you capture anything and everything your brain might consider you've committed to doing, at whatever time in the future and however loosely.

Make sure that whatever you use to record this, it's easily accessible. On the train, in bed, near the shower…! The more quickly you're able to fetch anything that pops into your head, the more organised and clear-headed you'll feel.

Step Two: O is for identify your Options

Most people skip this step and if you only take one thing away from my FOCUS Formula, I suggest you implement this. It will make a huge difference to how overwhelmed you feel.

When I was doing the research for my first book, I discovered some interesting things about overwhelm. Part of what makes us feel so stretched and leads down the road to burnout is not the activities themselves or even the number of them, but the lack of pauses between them. It's exhausting for our brains to jump from one type of activity to another, especially those that use different parts of our brains. Moving straight from 'ticking stuff off' type activities to creative ones and then back again with no pauses in between places a great deal of stress on our brains. It doesn't matter how long the pause is: it can be a few moments spent gazing out the window, putting the kettle on or simply allowing our minds to wander. The effect of these pauses is to reduce overwhelm and make us feel less stretched.

In a similar way, mixing up deciding with doing is exhausting. The second step in our FOCUS Formula is to decide on the first action associated with each item as you add it to your list. As an example, instead of simply writing 'Suzy' on your list, write 'Call Suzy about introduction to David'. Now you may think this is overkill – after all, when you see 'Suzy' on your list, you know why she's there. But every time you see 'Suzy' on your list, your brain has to quickly remember, often so quickly that you don't even notice, but the cumulative effect over hours, days and weeks can be significant.

I have a client who used to struggle with video creation for his fitness business. During one of our sessions, I asked him to describe the problem. He told me that he'd tried putting 'Videos' in a slot in his calendar, but every time he got to that slot, he would spend ages figuring out what he was trying to create, which footage to edit, what music to use and by the time he had figured all that out, he was out of time.

I got him to break down the process into steps and add them to his calendar, capturing brief notes on what he planned to do. What was amazing to watch was that something that had previously been taking him a good chunk of an hour could now be done in a matter of minutes. That's because previously his brain had been coming to the 'Video' slot expecting to do something and instead found that it had to make decisions. When his brain was in organising and scheduling mode, it was easy to quickly decide what his plan of action would be, safe in the knowledge that he didn't need to execute it until later. Now when he comes to those 'Video' slots in his calendar, they say 'Edit XYZ footage to create a video for ABC using HJK music.' No decision to make. Simply execute.

This is something I remind myself of often. Separate the deciding from the doing.

When you're considering your next action, always think of DDD:

- DO the task yourself now (if it will take you less than two minutes) or later.

- DITCH it altogether. Are you really going to do that task? By all means ditch it, but only if it's true. Don't forget your subconscious is part of your brain, so if you still intend, maybe, possibly, to do it one day, better keep it on the list.

- DELEGATE the task to someone else. Just because you can do something, doesn't mean you should. Who could you get to do it for you?

Step Three: C is for Categorise your lists

We've talked about clearing our head of everything and capturing our next action for each item, so now it's time to really get everything organised. In Step Three, we're looking at categories or buckets of tasks.

I like to organise all my actions and lists by themes. All the calls together, all the emails, all the things I want a particular member of the team to focus on. I also have what I call 'projects', collections of tasks that relate to a bigger goal. As an example, for my podcast project, I have a list of the people I would like to interview in one task. I have another with all the topics I want to talk about and a third contains my various notes of the tech I might need including software.

One of the reasons why it's important to group things together is it allows you to choose. One of the wonderful things about working for yourself is that you are able, to a certain extent, to choose what you spend your time on. So when you feel like doing something creative, you can turn to a category that contains that kind of task. Whereas if you're in need of the dopamine hit of ticking several things off in short succession, making a few calls or responding to a few emails might well do the trick.

One important last point before we leave Step Three. No general bucket. Do not allow one to creep in, even temporarily, as it represents the beginning of the slippery slope towards your brain no longer trusting that you're on top of everything. A general bucket requires you to switch between different types of tasks and will quickly become a dumping ground for anything you're not quite sure what to do with. If you can't decide where to put something, create a new bucket.

Step Four: U is for Understand your system

Talking of slippery slopes and our brain starting to consider stepping in and taking over again, Step Four is where you really need to keep up the discipline. If your system is going to fail, this is where it's likely to start. For your brain to trust you and stop trying to hold everything in memory, you have to have regular reviews of your system to keep on top of and understand what's in there.

On a daily basis, it's good to have a quick tidy-up. Cross off things that you've completed, move items added today into their rightful place. Use your calendar to plan things you're committing to doing in that time slot. If you find that you keep moving something around, it's either not a priority or you probably haven't followed Step Two and captured what the first step is to get it progressed. At the start or end of your day, decide what your top three things will be for that day or the next.

On a weekly basis, you need to schedule a more thorough review of your system. It's vital you keep it fresh and up to date. Clear out anything you've completed or decided not to do anymore. This is a Sunday afternoon or Monday morning type task, and if you skip it more than once or twice, you're already moving towards that slippery slope.

This is a powerful part of the process. If you think back to the last holiday you took, you probably made a list of things that needed to be done before you left. Maybe you got everything done or maybe you didn't, but there was almost certainly a moment in time when each and every item on your list was either ticked off or moved to a post-holiday list. Did you experience a wonderful moment, however brief, just as you left for your holiday when you felt totally organised and on top of everything? Maybe you didn't get everything done that you'd intended, but it was too late, you'd run out of time. It had to wait until you got back. The decks were completely clear, if only for a moment.

You thought you were feeling great because you were heading off on holiday, and I'm sure that was part of it. But you were also feeling great because your head was clear, you were organised, and everything was in its place for that one magical moment.

Step Five: S is for enjoy your Success

The last step is the result of all our efforts. The right action at the right time. Your head clear to make good decisions for you and your business.

In order for the FOCUS Formula to be effective, you must commit to performing all five steps consistently. Your system is personalised and adapted to your needs, but it must contain these five elements.

You must **fetch** everything. You must not add anything without considering your **options** and deciding on the next action. You must **categorise** into appropriate buckets so that your system remains flexible. You must **understand** what you have using daily and weekly reviews, and this all leads you to be able to enjoy the **success** that comes from taking action and doing the right things at the right time.

I have been using this system in various iterations for many years. When I was working in large organisations, I used to walk around with blank pieces of paper, usually the other side of the endless presentation decks and reports that seem to multiply in so many large organisations. I would keep four lists – one in each corner of my page. Things I needed to do or think about short term, things in the long term, things I needed to check with my teams, and things I needed to speak with my boss about. I would rewrite my list every time it got too messy.

When I started my own business, I moved to notebooks and the Notes app on my phone. I introduced software into the mix a few years ago. Some people get very excited about the tech, but in my experience, it's the process that's important. If you can't or won't follow the five steps of the FOCUS Formula, no software will be able to stop your brain intervening.

The most important principle is to keep things simple and efficient. The tool you decide to use is purely a personal choice.

CHAPTER 15

Growing Your Business

'Everyone wants to live on top of the mountain, but all the happiness and growth occurs while you're climbing it.'

— Andy Rooney, American radio and television writer[24]

One of the many changes that comes with running your own business is that you're always on the hunt for new clients. Anish describes it as a 'test of resilience'. He believes that you need to 'start experiencing rejection as early as possible, because it's only going to help you later on.'

Even if you get yourself into the fortunate position of people queuing up to work with you, where your next few clients are coming from will always be an important consideration. 'Having a robust pipeline

---

24 *The Complete Andy Rooney* (Warner Books, 1983)

is key,' Caroline told me. 'It allows you the band-width to hire your first team member and try new products.'

One of the things Tamara is concerned about is the 'relentlessness of moving forward. I feel like you can't just sit back and wait for opportunities to fall into your lap, like you sometimes can when you're employed. New clients and projects will come, but only if you keep proactively searching for them.'

If you start off doing all the delivery for your cli-ents, you'll have to split your time and headspace between serving the clients in front of you and main-taining a pipeline of prospects. Balancing delivery with business development is something you'll have to adjust to quickly. Sophie told me how she had to learn quickly to keep a healthy pipeline of clients. 'One December, I lost three clients in a week. All for very valid reasons. It was a coincidence.' We discussed the need for a backup plan. 'Never stop marketing,' she said. 'Keep the conversation going in the market, so people know who you are and what you do.'

Depending on your business, your future clients may come from a number of different sources. In this chapter, we'll look at some of the key sources of new clients and how to get them working for your business.

Referrals

A good habit to get into is to ask every person you speak to whom they might know that could benefit from a conversation with you. Every client should be asked for referrals during the time you're working together. Pick a moment that seems right with each client or plan it into your process so it's a formal step. I know people who have in their contracts with clients that referrals will be sought.

Don't forget to update your previous clients as you evolve your business and grow your offerings. It's easy to forget that not everybody is paying nearly as much attention to your business as you are.

Networking

Some people love networking, while for others it can feel daunting. There are many online groups both location- and sector-focused, so allow yourself the time to find the right one for you. Every person is a potential client or partner for you, so rather than thinking about trying to 'defend your territory', try and approach every conversation with an open mind.

Caroline's design agency business really started to grow when she took networking more seriously. 'It wasn't just all the other small businesses,' she told me, 'but the opportunities to buddy up and form joint ventures.' Before she built her team, she was able to pitch for broader pieces of work by collaborating with people who offered complementary services to her. 'Being able to white-label other services really helped me take my business to the next level.'

I regularly talk to 'competitors', share insights, offer support, and learn. My view is that there are so many people out there who need what I can offer, I cannot possibly hope to serve them all, so if I can help another coach in any way, I will. Another way of looking at this is that I'm not going to be a good fit with every potential client, and neither are you. Some people will be looking for exactly what you're offering, and others will be better suited to another provider. Your job is to serve and if that means matching a 'competitor' with a potential client who would be better suited to them then you've served both and done the right thing. Never make the mistake of believing you are the one and only solution.

Tamara has a similar mindset when it comes to networking. 'Many of the people I spoke with told me that, more often than not, other freelancers will be your collaborators rather than competitors. So far, I've found this to be true, and it's also great to meet others who are on a similar journey and can offer advice and camaraderie.'

Marketing

One of the biggest shifts we've seen in recent years is the way people buy and sell. We're checking out potential vendors and doing most of our due diligence online. When we hear someone mentioning a company or individual that might solve our problem, most of us will do a quick search before making contact. Depending on the type of purchase, your client might spend several hours online with you before you even know they exist. But as selling is all about building relationships with people, how do we do that when we don't even know who they are?

It's a common mistake to think that marketing is not important for a new business. As I mentioned earlier, your first few clients are likely to come from referrals and networking, so why do you need to spend money and time on marketing? There's still a 'build it and they will come' mentality among many new business owners, who inevitably face a rude awakening.

Have you ever wondered why household names spend a fortune on advertising? Everybody knows who they are, so what's the point? I heard it explained very well a few years ago. They're paying to occupy a tiny piece of your brain. They're spending money so that when I ask you to name a brand of sportswear, you'll tell me Nike or Adidas, without hesitating.

Your marketing needs to serve two purposes. First, when someone first hears about you, either because they get referred or they stumble across your name and they check you out online, they can find information that will make them feel that you 'get' the problem they're facing. They need to get a sense that you'll be able to help them understand the different options they can choose from and the pros and cons of each, and give them a clear outline of what you offer and how you can help them reach the outcome they want. And second, your marketing needs to help you occupy a piece of your potential client's brain so that if and when they face the problem you solve, you're the person they turn to. Sophie told me she couldn't count the number of times she's received requests for work the day after sending out a newsletter. 'It's about people remembering that you're there.' I have a similar experience with my weekly email. It encourages people to get in touch and when they need me, they think of me.

The 7–11–4 Formula

Most of us used to make buying decisions when standing in front of a selection of products and making a choice of which to buy. But all that has changed in recent years. Google published an ebook in 2011 called ZMOT (Zero Moment of Truth) which refers to the research phase that potential customers now go through before the seller becomes aware of them.

In Google's study they emphasised the importance of many points of contact with a potential customer. Their 7–11–4 Formula states that you need to have **seven** hours of interesting content available – blogs, videos, articles, books, podcasts – so people can spend time with you.[25] People need an average of **eleven** interactions with you before they'll buy, and **four** is the number of different media or locations that these interactions need to happen in: a face-to-face meeting, reading your book, article, blog, listening to you in an interview, or watching a presentation you're giving.

The good news is that if you follow this formula, most people you end up speaking with will be, to use marketing terminology, warm. It also means that the playing field is levelled, and the charismatic salesperson no longer has such an advantage. The challenge is figuring out how to take people through most of the sales process without speaking directly with them. You'll need a robust marketing effort to ensure that your pipeline of prospects stays consistently full.

This new way of buying means we need content to attract potential clients who are at each of the three phases of the buying process.

---

25   J Lecinski, 'Winning the Zero Moment of Truth', Google, www.thinkwithgoogle.com/_qs/documents/673/2011-winning-zmot-ebook_research-studies.pdf

The three phases of the buying process

Phase One – Awareness

During the first phase, our potential client is realising they have a problem. We're not trying to sell anything here. This is all about your content being educational and informative. It needs to attract your potential client's attention by using the words they would use to describe their problem and it needs to position you as an expert. Examples of types of content you could use include videos, blog posts, ebooks, reports, white papers, webinars, infographics, tools, checklists, how-to guides, and social media posts, covering trends in your industry and perspectives on the problems you solve.

Ask yourself:

- How would my potential clients describe their goals or challenges?

- How would they choose to educate themselves on these goals or challenges?

- What resources would be helpful for them at this stage?

Phase Two – Consideration

Next, our potential client is looking at options to solve their problem. Here we want to educate at a deeper level, engage our potential clients by providing insights and helping them evaluate options. We also want to discourage people who are not a good fit and point them in a better direction. Comparison guides work well here, as do case studies and social media posts talking about buying mistakes people make in this space.

Ask yourself:

- What types of solution might my potential clients consider?

- What are their options?

- How do they educate themselves about the various options?

- How do they decide which option is right for them?

Phase Three – Decision

Finally, our potential client has decided to buy a solution to their problem. Here we want to demonstrate that we can delight our potential clients by making it easy for them to buy from us. Demonstrations, free consultations and guarantees are winners here, as are case studies and step-by-step 'how to buy' guides.

Ask yourself:

- What criteria will my potential clients use to evaluate the different options?
- What makes my offering different?
- Who will be involved in the purchasing decision?

In my social media posts, I try to focus on being helpful and adding value, but also in helping people understand what it would be like to work with me.

There are many different marketing strategies you can employ. But in all of them, your message needs to be clear and to the point. What problem are you solving and who are you solving it for? You want to make it as easy as possible for potential clients to find you.

Funnels

Funnels have become all the rage, but in truth, they're simply a way of thinking about the journey described above. You don't just want to be easy to find, but easy to interact with. Most people's attention span is terrifyingly short, so we need to make it simple for people to feel that they're receiving value. What is it you want them to do next?

Most funnels start with an ad: an image, a video or a graphic that grabs the attention of your prospective client. Next, we want them to take some sort of action: click on a link, enter their details, watch or read something. At each stage of the process, we're offering value and building a connection. We're encouraging our potential client to spend time with us, perhaps by watching a webinar or attending an event or to make a small purchase, perhaps an entry-level product or the postage and packing on an otherwise free book. Once we're in a dialogue with them, we can invite them to engage with higher-value products and services.

In marketing, it's important to test, test, test. Put everything you think you know to one side and test. What headline grabs attention, what message is resonating, what images are working for you? Even the biggest brands in the world use paid advertising and as you look at growing your business, it's something you'll need to consider. My advice is to be organised. No point in testing several things at once. You need to be disciplined and change one thing at a time to truly know what works.

Your niche

Marketing experts will tell you that the *only* way to be successful is to niche. Most people who choose not to niche do so because they're scared of turning away business. In my case, I didn't want to niche because I wanted to serve business owners at different stages of growth. I wanted to meet people where they are. It's something I've wrestled with over the years.

It was only in the last two years that I really came to terms with who I am and what I do. I help people with transitions. The people who get attracted to me are all looking to make a change. Some are transitioning from employment to starting their own businesses. Others are realising that they need a proper management team to help them carry the load. Some are scaling their businesses and going through funding rounds, which requires their role as leader to evolve. Others are wanting to exit or step back from the day-to-day completely.

When thinking about your niche, it's important to keep in mind the problem you're solving and who you're solving it for, what sector they're in and at what stage of the journey they're on. As an example, if you're in training, are you helping people who are starting out or are you offering more expert guidance?

Nancy aims to find clients before they hit problems with their construction contracts. Her messaging is all about reading the contract upfront to avoid problems down the line. Katy usually meets her clients when they're already facing an investigation from HMRC and helps manage them through the process.

Some people pick a specific niche and others evolve theirs over time. I can't tell you what the right answer is. Certainly, I was successful before I defined my niche. I'm sure my marketing friends and colleagues would tell you that I could have been even more successful had I chosen a tighter niche earlier. One thing is certain, if you're struggling to cut through and find the clients you want to work with, then looking at your niche and ensuring you're talking directly to your target clients will certainly help.

A final word about marketing and in particular social media. Your online presence needs to be influenced by who you're planning to serve as clients. Anish shared with me that it took him more than a year before someone said to him, 'Your corporate clients really don't care what you put on LinkedIn. They're buying you and they want to believe you can solve the problem. It's in those business development calls where they will make that decision.' He spent a lot of time and energy on social media when he started out. He was focused on becoming more visible without really looking at how his potential clients were making buying decisions. 'You start looking at other people who aren't doing what you do, and you convince yourself that you've found a goldmine, a niche within a niche. It's really not as simple as that.'

It's easy to get swept up in the excitement and emotion of the entrepreneurial rollercoaster, which is why data and testing are vital. They keep you grounded and focused on what's real.

Sales

Selling makes many of us feel uncomfortable. Too many connotations of sleazy and aggressive car salespeople or unwelcome telesales calls. The truth is that many of us hate being sold to, but we love to buy! There are a few different reasons why you may have strong feelings about sales, and you may even believe things about sales that aren't true. Perhaps you've had negative experiences of being sold to, or maybe you've tried selling and struggled to do it successfully.

If you're someone who thinks they hate sales, it's likely you believe it's something you're doing to someone. Maybe you believe that selling requires you to convince someone to buy something they don't want or need or that they can't afford. The truth is that good selling is about helping your potential client make an informed decision about what to do and how to do it.

Like so many other aspects of running your own business, selling is a process that can be learned. Of course there are natural-born salespeople who build rapport easily, but if you're prepared to put the work in, anyone can learn to sell effectively and authentically.

The entire sales cycle may take several conversations or just a few minutes, depending on many different factors. In some cases, you may have to take your potential client through most of the process without speaking to them, as we looked at above, but there's no short-cutting the process. Every potential client will have to move through these three phases, in this order, before they'll consider signing with you.

Tool – The 3-Step Sales Process

There are three phases of selling and it's vital you don't move on to the next phase before you're really sure you're in full agreement with your potential client.

Phase One – The problem

The first phase is about agreeing with your potential client the problem they have and the urgency of that problem. They need to know that you understand, that you 'get' what they're struggling with. Until your potential client believes you understand their problem, they will not consider moving forward in the sales process. You also need to communicate and agree on the urgency. How critical is the problem and how quickly does it need to be fixed?

I meet many business owners who are frustrated with potential clients not buying, but that's because those clients are not feeling the pain or the urgency. You might be able to see why they need a solution right now, but unless and until they see it too, they will not buy.

Your job is to help them understand the potential implications of failing to act. Share your experiences – examples of people who failed to act in similar scenarios and case studies of people who did. Don't try to persuade; instead seek to educate. Rather than bombarding your potential clients with all the reasons why they need to act, try asking questions and seeking to understand their concerns. If you push too hard, you risk overwhelming them. If you fall into the trap of believing you know what's best for your potential clients, you're likely to put them off doing business with you.

Timescales are also important. You might be thinking of delivering your services this year, while your potential client might have in their mind some vague moment in the next five years. Don't make assumptions.

If you're in a conversation, you must summarise both the problem and the timelines and make sure you and your potential client are in agreement. Don't move on to Phase Two until you're sure you're on the same page. If you do, your potential client will not buy.

Phase Two – The potential solutions

This phase is the one that often gets missed. Most people will cover Phase One reasonably well and then move straight to Phase Three. This approach is likely to result in your potential client remaining stuck, unable to make a decision.

Here, you'll explore the different ways that our client might solve their problem. This is where you discuss the pros and cons of different kinds of solutions and gauge your potential client's views, experiences and preferences about each.

As an example, if your problem was that you wanted to understand how to transition from employment to running a business of your own, you have a number of options to choose from that would help you solve your problem. You might choose to buy a book or an online training programme. Or you might prefer a group programme or some one-to-one coaching. In this phase of the sales process, we're exploring with our potential client what type of solution is going to work for them. What's their experience been, if any, of learning from books or online, with group or individual coaching? What insights can you share about what works and what doesn't – and crucially, why?

We must focus on outcomes by painting a picture of the future. The biggest mistake I see at this stage of the process is that people jump into describing the solution that they offer when it's still too soon. The client is unlikely to buy if you jump in now. Focus on what kind of product or service will give them the outcome they want and why. Do they think that a structured process where they are taken step by step will work for them? Or would they be better suited to a do-it-yourself model where they move at their own pace and figure it out themselves? Focus on what *they* are looking to achieve.

This might happen in one or more conversations. It's important not to rush them. If you've done Phase One correctly and reached an agreement, then you're already on the same page about the timelines and urgency. By all means remind them of what they told you, but don't try to renegotiate timelines here.

Phase Three – Your offering

Only once you've agreed on the type of solution that will achieve the outcome they want can you move on to the third and final phase of the sales process. In an ideal world, I would try to stay in Phase Two until your potential client asks you how you would go about offering what they need. If that happens, then you know for sure that your potential client is ready.

Phase Three is where you talk about how you'll solve the problem your potential client is experiencing. This is where you can (finally) talk about how you work, the way you deliver the outcome they want. Give them some examples of people you've worked with and point out what makes your approach different. You'll know when you've done the first two steps right, because the sale becomes easy. You're offering your potential client the opportunity to buy from you, rather than being sold to.

At the end of the three phases, assuming you've gone through each of them properly, and you've reached agreement after each step, then there are only two reasons why your potential client won't say 'yes'. Either they don't trust you or they don't trust themselves. This is when they'll talk about price or timelines, and they'll tell you they're going to think about it. Your challenge is to figure out which person they don't trust and help them turn it around.

If they don't trust you, then they're worried you won't be able to deliver what you promise. Perhaps they need some sort of guarantee, more social proof or evidence. If they don't trust themselves, then they're worried about making a bad decision. Maybe they're struggling with confidence or doubt their ability to be able to apply themselves and put in the work required. Depending on your expertise, you may or may not be able to help them with this, but examples and proof can often help here too.

The most important skills in selling are asking great questions and listening. Your job is not to persuade but to serve your potential client by helping them make the best decision for them.

Tracking

Another significant decision you'll make early on is what to track in your business. You'll have an eye on the numbers of course, but it's also important to track activity. Business development will be a key area for you to monitor your progress, figure out what's working and adjust accordingly. Every time you sign a new client, make a note of what route they came through and ask yourself what you could do to replicate all or part of the circumstances that made them aware of you, get to know you and finally sign with you.

A very simple way of thinking about tracking your sales is in 'LAPS':

- **Leads** – any new name you become aware of who has the potential of becoming a client

- **Appointments** – any meaningful discussion about doing business (not just a chat!)

- **Proposals** – when you give details of your approach and pricing (always good to put it in writing)

- **Sales** – the deal is closed, the client has agreed to pay

These categories may not exactly fit your business but see if you can adapt them to suit your needs. Tracking these four things means you won't go far wrong.

Although your first clients will likely come from your network and referrals, it's important to think about how you're going to attract more clients, especially if you have aspirations to grow your business. The cost of acquisition is an important metric to track and needs to feed back into your pricing as you refine your offerings.

Clients

You've put a lot of effort into doing your research, understanding your market and getting your messaging right. You've taken your clients through the whole sales process, answered all their questions and managed the negotiations. By the time you sign a new client, you absolutely want it to work. Your clients pay you for your services. Without them you have no income, no business, no freedom.

Having said all that, how do you ensure you're not dancing to their every tune, that they don't take over your life? How do you serve them in ways that still work for you and your business?

Clients are the lifeblood of any business. Everyone knows that no business could exist if it didn't take care of them. But *managing* your clients is just as important as managing suppliers or members of your team, and if you aren't careful, they can end up causing you unneeded stress and consuming valuable time.

Managing expectations is vital, especially when you're a small business servicing large ones. According to Andy, being more flexible and nimbler will only get you so far. 'When a large organisation wants to do things their way, be it governance, structure, or number of meetings, you often just have to conform to it.' If your clients are large corporates, you don't get to escape that life completely. 'My team are still having to do the thing I've moved away from.'

Sophie spoke about the mindset shift that's needed to have meetings with potential clients. 'It's not the same as an interview. You're not going in there all eager-beaver, saying you can do everything,' she told me. 'You're listening to what they say and you're offering solutions. This is how I would do it if you were to engage my services. This is the value I offer.' She learned this through coming out of a meeting, realising it hadn't gone well and adjusting her approach in the next one.

For some, the most challenging thing about running their own business is having to turn down work. 'It's a very privileged position to be in,' one interviewee told me. 'But it's horrendous. A feeling of dread. Will work ever come back to me if I turn this down? And also a feeling of letting someone down.' We talked about reframing that dread and focusing on serving a few clients well rather than trying to serve everyone and ending up doing a subpar job.

The most important thing is to be honest with yourself about what you can and can't offer, what will work for you and what won't. Toxic productivity is just as much of a risk in small businesses as in large ones.

Seven tips on managing your clients

Here are a few ideas of how to set boundaries with your clients.

1. **Have clear working hours.** When are you off the clock? It isn't healthy to be available to clients 24/7. Spend some time deciding what your 'on'

hours are going to be. Let your clients know when you'll be available. You can assure them that they can email you whenever a question pops up, but you won't be answering it outside of working hours. Consider limiting calls and texts to those same hours.

The great part about working for yourself is that you can work additional hours if you need to. You may end up working one weekend when you're slammed. And that's OK. It happens. You just don't want your clients to expect you to be accessible to them all the time.

Most clients will totally understand. If you have one that doesn't, it may take a little extra time to educate them. You might have to spend some time assuring this type of client that it's OK, that you haven't forgotten about them, and you absolutely are going to finish the project on time. They will eventually get used to you having specific hours of availability.

I have one client who puts her 'out of office' on over the weekend. It clearly says, 'I'm not working until Monday, your email will get read then.'

2. **Set emails to delay send.** This is something I've implemented in the last year and it's made a huge difference to me and my business. Only send emails during your working hours and if you're working at other times, set your emails to send

later. This is especially useful for those needy clients you might be trying to educate.

Although some of your clients might take getting an email from you on the weekend as you putting in a little extra time, others will take it as an invitation to contact you whenever they want and expect you to respond.

3. **Take time for yourself.** All work and no play is a recipe for burnout. If you're always working, you won't have any time for ensuring your own needs are met. Then difficult clients without boundaries will be even harder to handle with tact and grace. It's a downward spiral that you must break.

   Give yourself time to relax. Grab a cup of coffee and relax while you drink it. Head to the gym. Watch a couple of episodes of your favourite Netflix addiction. Schedule time to refresh yourself regularly. Taking time to fill your own cup also improves your self-worth. You'll realise that you are a valuable person, and don't need to be available for every whim of your clients. You have the right to establish boundaries.

4. **Be aware of scope creep.** Sometimes clients don't overstep boundaries right away. Often, it's a simple request here, or an urgent upgrade thrown in there. But these little requests add up, and before you know it, you're doing more than your contract stipulated, without getting additional compensation.

Scope creep is real, so you must be on the lookout for it. Be sure you've clearly defined the details of the project for your client. And get your contract signed so both parties agree to the scope of the project. When requests come up that aren't part of that original agreement, you can decide if it's something you want to allow, or if you'll need to charge additional for it. Unfortunately, the line between offering excellent customer service and being taken advantage of often blurs. You'll have to pinpoint what your personal boundaries will be.

5. **Set expectations.** Most pushy clients simply don't realise they're overstepping boundaries. This is especially true if you've let them in the past. If you've always responded to every request within minutes, they're going to expect that to continue, until you put an end to it.

That's why communication is essential. Talk to your clients about your expectations and need for personal time. Address concerns about scope creep before you get frustrated. You aren't going to lose most of your clients because you establish boundaries. In fact, they'll probably respect you more once you start respecting yourself. Any client you do lose is one that wasn't worth having in the first place. Remember that not every client is a good client, and establishing boundaries is one way to cull out the bad ones.

6. **Get rid of hostile clients.** Your time is valuable. There's no reason you should use up all your time talking on the phone to people who are hostile, unruly, or who clearly have no intention of becoming your client.

   Business owners who offer truly exceptional customer service will be tempted to endure even the worst callers. Without a doubt, it's admirable to provide this level of service; however, you should not feel obligated to tolerate people who are making you or your team miserable. Be polite and simply send them on their way.

   There may be exceptions, of course, as in the case of a high-profile client that you may deem it necessary to tolerate. It's up to you how much you're willing to endure to secure a client or a sale. Remember that you're essentially giving them tacit permission to treat you badly though, and they may continue to do so if they can get away with it.

7. **Beware people who just like to talk.** In addition to hostile clients, there are also people who just want free information, without any plans to buy from you. Though it's a good thing to provide comprehensive information to potential clients, plenty of other callers may be waiting, who *are* planning on buying.

   No self-respecting lawyer would give away free legal advice to someone they know isn't going to use their services, and though you don't have to be as unforgiving as they might be, you may want to cut someone off if they're always calling and never buying. Naturally, you don't want to develop a reputation for being a tyrant, but simply to be pragmatic and sensible about your boundaries. The goal is not to alienate your clients, but anyone visiting or calling a business expects it to operate within a reasonable structure.

Don't be afraid to maintain consistent standards. As long as you show respect for your clients and take care of them, they will respect the fact that you run things on your own terms. This is the kind of client you want.

One of the best things about working for yourself is that you get to choose the types of people you work with – who you have in your team and what clients you want to work with. Think about your current best client, the one you and your team love working with. What makes them the best? Is it the way they behave, the problem you solve for them or are they the most profitable? How did they find you? Get really clear on everything about them, how you interact with each other and what makes it work. Then you can start thinking about how to find more clients like them. The real magic is that the clearer you get, the more likely you are to attract exactly who you'd ideally like to work with.

CHAPTER 16

The Reality

'The only thing we have to fear is fear itself.'
— Franklin D Roosevelt, 32nd president of the United States[26]

Starting, running and growing a business is hard. Being an entrepreneur can feel like being in a car with no brakes on an icy road. It can be overwhelming, infuriating and exhilarating all at the same time. The ability to get back up when you've been knocked down is an important trait for anyone to develop, but for entrepreneurs, it's vital.

Being an entrepreneur isn't for everyone. There are no guarantees, and many people give up or fail. But running your own business and being in control of

---

26 Inaugural address, Washington DC, 4 March 1933

how you spend your time is fantastic. Many people, including me, couldn't imagine doing anything else.

Most people don't move outside their comfort zone or take too many risks. They settle for average or easy and that's absolutely their right. We all have moments of doubt. We all second-guess ourselves from time to time. But if you want to build a business, you'll need to be prepared to work hard and back yourself, even in those dark moments when nothing seems to be going right.

For Nancy, it's not just about having the self-belief but developing it: 'You've got to take the knocks and you've got to keep going.' Sophie's advice is, 'Don't get comfortable. You never know what's round the corner.'

One of the greatest gifts that can come from working for yourself is the ability to spend time with yourself, understanding your rhythms, your ups and downs, what gives you energy and what drains you. We all have cycles, some more pronounced than others, but when you're in control of your own schedule, you have the opportunity to build it around you and your specific needs. Are there times of the day, week and month where you're fresher and more energised? Are there activities you need to prepare for and others that need a certain headspace? If you take the time to understand yourself, you can focus on building the type of business that will work for you.

In this chapter, we'll explore some of the realities of running your own business.

Eight working from home tips

If you're used to going into an office every day, you may find learning how to organise yourself to work from home challenging. You may have learned a lot during the pandemic, but here are some tips:

1. **Get dressed.** Yes, this is one of the biggest luxuries of working from home. It's beautiful to be able to walk from the bedroom to the office in your pyjamas to turn on the computer, walk downstairs with bed hair to make coffee, and make a conference call before brushing your teeth. But it's important to cue your body and mind to move from 'home' to 'work'. You don't need to get into your best suit. Wear something comfortable, but at least choose something that makes you feel you're working.

2. **Create a workspace.** Don't work in bed or on the sofa. Get a grown-up chair and table that's used only for your work. Find a space where you can get peace, quiet and privacy. Get the supplies and equipment that you need to be efficient and comfortable. If possible, make the space separate and different from the rest of your home. If you can create a boundary for your workspace, you'll also be setting up a home space by default. If

you're taking your laptop all around the house to work, your family or friends will feel that no place is safe from your work. At the same time, don't allow the people you live with to take over your office space. It should be clutter-free, or at least only cluttered with work stuff.

3. **Set office hours.** These don't have to resemble normal business hours. They can start at 2am and end at noon. They can be in two-hour blocks with one-hour breaks to attend to personal matters. They can change on a daily basis. But having a schedule with your set office hours will let your family, team and clients know when you're working and when you're available for them. Take advantage of your flexible schedule to take a few hours off to do the things you love. Make a to-do list with your family and friends, so you can plan and look forward to spending as much time with them as possible outside of your conference calls and deadlines.

4. **Don't mix.** Set parameters around doing personal tasks during the day. There are a lot of errands and chores that we have to take care of when running a household. Trips to the supermarket, laundry to be done, dishes to be put away or a garden that needs tending. The beauty of working from home is that you're less restricted by when you need to do those things. But if you take work time to do home stuff, you'll just as easily take home time to do work stuff. It's perfectly fine to work for two hours and then take a one-hour

break to clean the house, if that's the schedule you've decided on. Just make sure that you're not jumping back and forth haphazardly.

5. **Keep hydrated.** You might not even notice you're thirsty, but before you know it, you've gone six hours straight on no food or water. If you don't take care of your health while you work, you won't fully be present when you're with your friends and family. All of a sudden, you'll realise how exhausted you are. Also, drinking plenty of water will force you to get up and walk to the bathroom, so you're not literally glued to your chair for hours.

6. **Take breaks.** Schedule them at a certain time or after a certain task, but make sure you schedule them. It gets you into the habit of stopping work. If you just take a break whenever you feel like it, you'll find that you won't feel like it too often. But if you take your specified breaks, the idea of letting work go at the end of the day won't be so hard. You'll learn that work will still be there when you get back, and that it's OK to stop working to do something less 'important'.

7. **Go outside.** In the confines of your small home office, it's difficult to see beyond your work. Make sure to get some real-world time every day, even if it's just to walk outside for ten minutes. Get some sun, smell the fresh air. There's no better way to quickly get some perspective. There's a lot of life to live. Remember what and who you're

working so hard for, and make sure you don't miss any of it.

8. **Have a trigger for winding down.** Many employees are eagerly watching the clock at the end of the day. They know they have to start finishing things up for the day by a certain time so they can leave on time. They're prepared to do what they can today and finish it off tomorrow. For those who work from home, this is an extremely difficult thing to do. The computer is always within reach. It's always possible to get back to work and get more things done. If you have an office you need to leave, it's easier to separate work life from home life. But when your work is at home, it's always in competition. Do I watch TV with my husband or work on that project? It shouldn't be an option, though. You need to develop cues to help you wind down and let the work go until tomorrow. Decide on a time every day to close out your email. Write up notes on things to do tomorrow and plan out your next day. These are things that will help you leave work for when you're next back at your desk. Also, it will remove any guilt you might feel about stopping work for the day.

You and your health

One of the things I've learned over the years is just how important my health is. I've also learned a lot about stress. I used to think that stress only came from negative things, tasks or situations you didn't like. As I've generally been lucky enough to love what I do, I spent years not realising how stressed I was. Now I understand that stress comes from pushing too hard, not taking breaks between activities and from asking yourself to carry a lot. I know now that stress can be good if you manage it well. But I've had to learn the hard way.

My story: 'Why don't you take a book and go and sit by the beach for a couple of hours?'

Have you ever had a time in your life when you're so stressed or broken, you hardly recognise yourself?

When I first started my coaching business in 2017, I attacked it with all the energy and enthusiasm I'd shown throughout my career. I wanted to learn everything I could and move fast. I soon attracted some great clients and threw myself into serving them. I was working longer and longer hours, struggling to switch off and the list of things I wanted to get done was growing longer by the day.

In March 2018, I was invited to go to Dubai to run a workshop for a cohort of MBA students. I was in my hotel room with the blinds drawn to keep the bright sunshine out and I was hunched over the desk. Suddenly a message from my sister popped up on the screen.

Are you still working? it said.

I stopped what I was doing. I'd been caught out!

Are you working London and Dubai hours? the message continued.

This was my middle sister. Long brown hair and beautiful eyes. I could picture her frowning at me, concern in her eyes. *I should probably answer her,* I thought. *She knows I'm here.*

Why don't you take a book and go and sit by the beach for a couple of hours?

Have you ever been in a situation when someone's talking to you, and you haven't a clue what they're talking about? Book? Beach? I didn't actually know what she meant. *Why would I read a book? What did she mean by beach? I don't have time for all that,* I thought.

I didn't answer her message and I didn't go to the beach, but her words kept popping into my head. That night I couldn't sleep. My mind was racing. *Am I losing the plot? How come I didn't know Dubai was by the sea? How did I not even understand what she meant when she suggested I take a couple of hours off? What's wrong with me? How do I get some balance in my life? I know I'm working too hard, but I love it, so what's the harm?*

Over the weeks that followed, the nagging fears and doubts grew. I noticed myself making mistakes and forgetting things. I struggled to sleep and then would wake up exhausted. I couldn't make decisions about food, so just ate the same thing day after day. The voice in my head saying, *You're working too hard, you're working too hard* got louder and more insistent.

One day, I had an epiphany. I could get a personal trainer and he could come to me. We could train by the water near my flat and I could improve my health that way. And that was why I found myself meeting Gabriel bright and early on the morning of 26 July 2018. I was bright-eyed and bushy-tailed and delighted with my decision to take better care of myself.

It was a free introductory session and he was really putting me through my paces, keen to impress me so that I would become a regular client. I hadn't done any exercise for several years, but I was loving moving my body. We were doing all kinds of cardio and core exercises, and by the end of the hour I was feeling amazing and really pleased with myself.

By the time I arrived back at my apartment, I could hardly walk. I didn't know what was happening, it felt like my whole body was shutting down. I got myself into the shower on autopilot, but my whole body was going into shock. I couldn't stand, so I slid down to the floor of the shower cubicle, but there wasn't enough space. I really needed to lie down. I staggered into the bedroom and collapsed on the floor. I was having a strange out-of-body experience. I was on the floor, soaking wet, shaking like a leaf. I wasn't scared. *Why am I not scared?* I wondered. I just felt really sad. How could I have let myself get into such a state?

Within fifteen minutes, I was feeling much better again and I was getting myself ready to head out when it hit me. *You're doing it again! You're ignoring what's going on. You're just going to power on through. How bad does it need to get before you'll pay attention? You didn't listen in Dubai and you're not listening now. How can you help anyone else if you won't help yourself?*

I made a deal with myself that day. In return for properly prioritising my health, I would stop nagging myself about how hard I work. I put a recurring daily one-hour 'Health' slot in my calendar, and I started educating myself about nutrition, sleep and wellness. I also learned an important lesson. It's so easy to tell ourselves that we're too busy, but time management is all about choices. We all have the same twenty-four hours in the day, and it's our choice what we spend them on.

Perhaps you're thinking I'm some sort of paragon of virtue, who's exercising every day because I enjoy it. I want to let you in to a secret. It's not actually that revolutionary, but I do wish someone had told me this much earlier in life. Moving your body changes everything. Whether you walk, run, cycle, practise yoga or swim, the positive impacts of having a regular exercise regime are profound and life-changing. I used to connect exercise with weight loss. I used to look at runners and wonder why they were running when they were already thin. Today, I'm still amazed that I can be feeling low, demotivated, sluggish, stressed, overwhelmed or anxious, and as long as I can persuade myself to move, it doesn't matter whether it's the treadmill, swimming pool or going out for a walk, the change in my mood is immediate. Unless you're unwell and need to rest, moving your body changes everything.

I totally get that vigorous exercise isn't for everyone, but I have to tell you that in the last few years, I've discovered that it's the greatest stress-buster I've ever experienced. I have a busy life. I work hard and I love what I do. But I expect a lot of myself and I want to move fast, so for me, vigorous exercise is a must. Every morning I feel as if the stress is literally pouring out of me, cleansing my system and preparing me for the day ahead. Moving my body enough that it makes me really sweat makes my brain feel like it's had a deep clean. Following a routine where everything's decided upfront is such an amazing relief. However stressed, anxious or busy I feel when I wake up, and whatever I have on my plate for the day ahead, by the time I'm finished, I feel ready to face whatever comes my way.

I'm also a woman of a certain age and if that's you too, you'll understand what I mean when I say that I want to prepare my body for what's to come. A few years ago, when I was in my mid-forties, I remember calling my mother and asking her how old she was when she went through menopause. When she told me she was about fifty-five, my heart sank. Ten more years of this? But now as I challenge my body and increase my strength and endurance, I feel fortunate to have discovered exercise in time to prepare myself for what's ahead.

I also love the mental challenge. I used to think that physical exercise was about the strength of my body, but discovering the power of my mind has been a revelation. I've always been fascinated by running, but at school I hated it. It made my chest hurt and no one ever taught me how to breathe properly. I've tried a couple of times as an adult but never persevered. I always felt weak and feeble and frustrated by how slow I was. When I broke my ankle in 2002 and had metal plates inserted, I thought that was it for any aspirations I had to be a runner. I was encouraged to try it and discovered that if you strengthen your body, you'll run faster. But I was still frustratingly slow and couldn't run more than three kilometres.

I went out one morning with my husband, who'd been running for years. At the time we lived in the Docklands in East London and there was a perfect pavement to run on in a figure eight all around the beautiful dock. It was a struggle to keep up with him but a relief to let someone else set the pace. At the 3k point, when I thought he would head for home, he suddenly turned and headed for the upper loop. I was so exhausted, I couldn't think straight or make a decision, so I just went with it. And that was my first 5k run.

I'd been convinced that I couldn't run that far, but it turned out I was wrong. It made me think about all the things we tell ourselves we can't do when actually we can. Everything is impossible until it's not. When I'm in the gym and my brain tells me that a weight is too heavy, I repeat inside my head, *I am strong. I am strong!* and my body lifts it.

If you've never been a fan of exercise, trust me, I do understand. I've never been sporty and I hated gym at school. All I can say is, why not give it a go? Try it out and see what it can do for you. Find your own balance and rhythm but please, prioritise your health.

I've never gone back on the deal I made with myself, and I never will. I've come to understand that without exercise, I wouldn't be able to do what I do. Without my health, I have nothing. Without my health, I *am* nothing.

Think about your non-negotiables. What are the things you want in your life, regardless of what else you have on your plate?

Learning as you go

For many people, the ability to learn and discover new things is one of the best aspects of working for themselves. It's something they really value. For Austin, running his own business 'creates the opportunity to develop so many different skills. It's definitely more of a vocation than a job.' He told me, 'If everything's in harmony, there's a real chance of having a business and never working another day in your life!'

For me, the journey of self-exploration and self-awareness has been profound. It's had excruciating lows full of self-doubt and loathing and highs of unbelievable exhilaration and joy.

My story: 'I bet you've never felt completely overwhelmed and frustrated, Lisa!'

It was April 2018 and I was on a video call with someone I'd met in the early days of my business. Her face was usually lit up by a beautiful smile but today she looked frustrated and sad.

'Oh, Lisa – I know I've only just met you, but I just need to share this with you,' she said. 'To be honest, I've had enough, and I feel so guilty. This business is important to me, it's something I really believe in. I can't believe I'm telling you all this. I'm sorry. You seem so organised and sorted, I'm probably not making any sense.'

You know that feeling when someone says something to you, and in your head you're thinking *Oh my God, you couldn't be more wrong!*? I know I can come across as a bit of a superwoman: organised, capable and focused. But as she was talking, I was remembering the many times I'd wanted to walk away from my business. When I'd been so overwhelmed and frustrated that I just didn't know which way to turn. When I'd been plagued by self-doubt – *Who's going to listen to you, Lisa?* When I had to justify to people around me why I was walking away from my well-paid job to work with small business owners.

'I can assure you that I've had my moments too,' I said. 'Contrary to popular belief, we're all human, including me, and I certainly have my ups and downs. But I'd love to know, what do you enjoy about what you do?'

She gave me a big smile. 'I love training and talking to people. I love getting out there and spreading the word.'

'What is it that you don't enjoy so much?'

Her beautiful face screwed up into a sad frown. 'Errrghhh! I just can't stand all the admin, all the HR stuff, all the IT and tech – it drives me crazy and it drains me. I've got so much I want to do but I never get the time. I just don't know what to do! I'm falling out of love with my business. I feel so stuck. I just think the only way for me is to close down and start something new.'

I believe that if we're really present and we listen, the universe always brings us what we need. Patterns in our lives are a result of us not learning. If we don't have that difficult conversation, if we walk away instead of facing our challenges, the universe, the world, our higher self – whichever way you want to look at it – will find a way to present us with that same lesson once more. This is why we can move from one relationship to another and, however different the new relationship may seem at the start, the same challenges will start appearing. This is the reason why you might face a series of difficult bosses or needy friends. Instead of focusing on them or on why this is happening 'to' you, the question to ask yourself is, 'What can I learn here? What is in my power to change?'

One of the things that many coaches, consultants and therapists learn over the years is that our clients bring us what we need. This 'chance' conversation helped me see my path forward. At the time I was feeling completely overwhelmed and close to burnout. In the process of coaching her I was able to see that I was also in danger of falling out of love with what I was doing.

In the months that followed, I helped her get organised. We streamlined those tasks that she didn't enjoy so they took up less time. I helped her put in boundaries for herself and she got back some of her mojo. She had more time to focus on what she loved, which was creating new products and training. But she was still frustrated and she wanted things to move quicker. One day she told me she wished she could hire me. It's always flattering when someone offers you a job and it's something you may have to watch out for. It happens fairly frequently in my line of work, and I always make sure I tell my client how grateful I am and how I'm taking it as a big compliment. The truth is, I can add so much more value to their business as their coach rather than as an employee.

This was the first time a client had offered me a job. 'You're a brilliant implementer, Lisa,' she told me. 'I just want things to be done, but you know how to get them done!'

When she said that, it catapulted me back almost fourteen years to the nineteenth floor of a tower block in Delhi, India. I was with my boss, a serious man who was not to be messed with! He often had a frown on his face, but on the day that I was remembering – a very hot and sticky July day – he was laughing. Out loud. At me.

He'd just asked me what my plans were once my two-year assignment ended that autumn. 'Will you stay in India or go back to London, Lisa?'

'I'm going to go back to London and look for another job. I'm going to have to leave Xerox. There's no place for me here – I'm just not one of those people and I never will be.'

You see, even though I was very successful and well regarded, I lived in fear of being found out. One day someone would come and tell me that I didn't belong.

That I wasn't creative, charismatic, visionary enough to progress any further.

My boss was laughing. 'Whatever do you mean?' he asked between chuckles.

Have you ever been in a situation when you thought, *This person isn't taking me seriously!*? What about that feeling where hot tears of anger and frustration start pricking at your eyes? I was feeling shame, guilt and confusion, and suddenly I was annoyed with myself for even mentioning it.

He immediately stopped laughing. He could see that I was upset. He looked at me and his eyes were kind.

'You're amazing, Lisa! Just look at everything we've achieved together here in India! I wouldn't have got anything done here if it wasn't for you. You are such a great implementer. Every single one of those creative, charming, strategic people you talk about need someone like you! They would give their right arm to work with you. You are such a valuable part of this company – please don't leave.'

It was a life-changing moment for me. When my client said she wanted to hire me, that clarity came flooding back. I didn't go and work for her, of course, but what I did do was encourage her to find her very own implementer. And a few months later we all met up together with the team and it was all happiness and smiles, until I said to my client, 'Tell her what you told me in the car', and she gave me such a look. You know that look you give your partner or your friend, or that they give you – yeah, one of those!

She had picked me up from Oxford station a few hours beforehand, beaming and waving out of the car window.

'How's your new lady doing?' I asked her.

'Oh she's just great! I feel like I've got a complete team now – the four of them work so well together. I just wish I could give her everything! I just feel so guilty dumping everything on her and I don't want to overload her.' She definitely wasn't planning on saying any of that in this meeting – so the look she shot me was like, 'I thought you were supposed to be *my* business coach!'

It was one of those situations where you're put on the spot by someone and it makes you feel a bit uncomfortable even though you know their intentions are good and they want the best for you.

'Trust me – just tell her!' I said gently, and then it all came pouring out.

'You're doing such a great job and I don't want to overload you and...' she trailed off.

'Just tell her.'

'I really just want to hand over everything – all the day-to-day stuff.'

Her implementer was sitting there in her white collar, exuding calm confidence, notebook at the ready. I turned to her with a smile and asked her to respond.

'Bring it on!' she said with a big, beaming smile.

My client looked like all her dreams had come true, all her birthdays and Christmases rolled into one. The next day, she sent me a message saying she'd woken up with no back pain for the first time in several months.

What I learned that day is one of the most important things I've ever learned about running a business. I call it the Entrepreneur Triangle, which is something that every entrepreneur and business owner needs to understand.

The Entrepreneur Triangle

I'm a simple soul at heart and for me, everything that happens in a business can be divided into three categories.

First, there's the core skill – that thing you're good at. Maybe you're an engineer or a creative artist. Perhaps you have set of technical skills or you're great with people. You may be an accountant or a marketeer.

Then there are all the *out* elements of a business – attracting clients, generating interest, sales and marketing, investors, partnerships, building your brand and communicating your message.

And finally, there are all the *in* activities – operational and administrative tasks, all the nuts and bolts, finances, legal, hiring people and managing people.

To start a business, you must obviously have the first. But the thing that I've learned throughout my career and what my client and her new implementer reminded me of that day is that most people are good at one of the other two, but not both.

What I want you to take away is that whatever you choose to build in terms of a business, whether you're aiming for world domination, or a simple business based on you serving your clients, you're going to need help. You can't be good at everything. When you start, you need to have a handle on everything. But you can't be both a champion and an implementer. For every Steve Jobs, there's a Steve Wozniak and for every Mark Zuckerberg, there's a Sheryl Sandberg.

You might be wondering what happened to me when I left India. I started my own business but not straight away. I did go back to London, and I did stay with Xerox. I trained as a Lean Six Sigma Blackbelt which is a fine title for an implementer! My Mum used to tell her neighbours that her daughter was training to be a ninja. ('You do know it's a project management qualification don't you, Mum?' 'Well yes, dear and I'm very proud of you.') You know when you're trying to explain what you do to someone who's not quite getting it?

In 2014, I got headhunted into an investment bank, an industry I knew nothing about. I started off running a small project and ended up as the right-hand woman of the head honcho, managing large teams and multidiscipline programmes. One day, my boss asked to see me.

'I need you to manage a new project for me – the regulators are breathing down my neck and I can't trust anyone else to get it over the line for me.'

'What's it all about?' I asked.

'You'll figure it out,' he told me with a smile.

But I didn't really need to. I had half a floor full of credit officers on one side and some seriously intelligent quants on the other side. I didn't need to know the ins and out of the subject matter. They knew more about it then I could even begin to fathom. But I knew how to manage people, organise and get things done and meet deadlines.

On my last day in the bank, when I'd decided to leave and support my husband in his new business, a lady approached me at my leaving drinks. 'When you first joined, I couldn't understand why he'd hired you,' she told me. 'Why would he hire someone who knew nothing about credit risk, who didn't even have a background in banking? But now I've seen what you've managed to achieve and all the projects we've got over the line with your help. Now I get it. I didn't know people like you existed. Thank you.'

If you ever find yourself doubting yourself or thinking, *I can't give that task to anyone else – it's boring and I would feel guilty. How can I give something to someone else that I would hate to do myself?*, please remember my story. Every creative person needs an implementer, and every person has their own superpower, even if it can take some time to figure out exactly what it is.

Being your own boss is not without its challenges, of course. Instead of having a defined role, with a manager and a structure, it's up to you to decide when and how hard you work. From the outside, this sounds like a dream, but the reality is that it can be a challenge to manage yourself. Rather than looking to others to assess and critique you, deciding whether you're worth a promotion or a pay rise, you'll have to decide for yourself. Rather than getting feedback from your manager, if you're lucky, you'll have to ask your clients and interpret what the market is telling you.

Finding ways to keep your motivation and confidence up is crucial. A great strategy is to focus on evidence rather than results. Keep a record of the small things, the indicators that you're moving in the right direction. A positive comment from a prospective client, an article about your area of expertise that confirms you're on the right track, an introduction to a new prospect, an achievement of a small goal you've set yourself. It takes many steps to reach the end goals like money in the bank and freedom to plan your time. Start noticing all those tiny steps, the crumbs along the way to *your* definition of success.

One of the great challenges but also joys of running your own business is all the new things you get to experience and learn. Nancy told me that something that was really important to her when she started out was 'being in control of the training and learning that I do, and how I develop and grow.' She invested in several different training courses in areas she wanted to master and found that she got so many useful insights that she could apply to her particular niche.

You can be whoever you want to be. It will take time, effort and dedication, but your future is in your own hands.

Consistency

Most people can have one good call or meeting, one good pitch or presentation. Most people can raise the bar and excel every now and then. But doing so consistently is something special.

One of the most important – and difficult – lessons I've learned on my business journey is that it's not the smartest or most organised or most talented people who succeed. It's the ones who show up and do their thing, day in, day out, consistently. One of my mentors once told me, 'Being average consistently will always beat being amazing sporadically.' This idea offended me then and it still offends me today, but he was so right.

Consistency means the people around you – your team, your clients, your investors – know what to expect. You are reliable. And whenever people trust you, space is created for opportunities. Consistency means that your brain doesn't go into panic mode. It means that you keep your promises to yourself, whether it be around family time, health goals or your business. Consistency means that you prioritise doing what will lead you to where you want to be, rather than allowing yourself to be distracted by all the 'shiny-shiny'.

Developing consistency actually goes against human nature. It takes energy and patience. It can be mastered, but it takes practice. You need to replicate positive behaviour or performance until it defines you.

Top ten consistency tips

1. **One goal.** Pick one goal to focus on at a time. Otherwise you'll get overwhelmed and give up. What's your biggest issue or most damaging inconsistency? Start with that and get it stable before moving on.

2. **Increments.** Focus on small, incremental improvements. It won't happen overnight. It takes time and effort and energy and perseverance. Celebrate your achievements along the way, however small, to keep yourself motivated.

3. **Fight.** We naturally avoid things that are hard. Your brain will tell you you're tired, that you don't have to do it today, that you can have a day off. Don't fall for it. Push through and build a new habit. Otherwise you'll be back to square one.

4. **Be kind.** You will fall off the wagon and that's OK. Tomorrow is another day. Be kind to yourself. Yes, you need to fight, but being too hard on

yourself is counterproductive. Getting back on track quickly is key.

5. **Use routines.** Deciding what you're going to do, wear, eat ahead of time is hugely powerful. Having a positive start and end to the day makes you feel in control and helps you embed positive practices.

6. **Be intentional.** Build a system around what you want. Routines, people, tasks, tools – everything needs to support your goals. If it's not aligned then get rid of it. Avoid distractions. Focus is key.

7. **Avoid self-doubt.** It's the ultimate consistency-destroyer. Trust the system, the process that you've designed to get you to your goal. Then get your head down and do the work. Only after you've done the work should you review your progress.

8. **Decide.** We are what we do, so you need to decide to be a person who does XYZ consistently. It needs to define you. It needs to be who you tell yourself you are. It's a decision and you need to decide.

9. **Improve.** One of the things about consistency is that it's boring. Especially if you like variety. Your creativity yearns for an outlet and all this consistency keeps getting in the way. So keep improving. Be consistent at improving.

10. **Enjoy.** If this all sounds like a lot of hard work, that's because it is. But that doesn't mean you can't enjoy the process. Review your progress, celebrate and then move on to the next goal.

Austin's been in business for eleven years. He told me you need to be ready to work harder than you've ever done and not to expect success overnight. 'Understand that success comes from applying yourself daily,' he said. He suggested allowing three years to really figure things out: the first to set up, the second to confirm, the third to triangulate.

There's no denying that having the ability to define what 'good' looks like is a plus point in many people's eyes. One of my interviewees talked about how important it was to 'be able to fulfil my own idea of what good service is.'

With so many distractions and opportunities, it can be a challenge to stay focused. The grass often looks greener, but my advice is to pick a lane and stay in it.

The cycles we run

Just because you've left the world of employment doesn't mean that you won't face similar challenges. You're still you after all! We all have different patterns or cycles that we run, and you'll need to watch out for yours.

I mentioned toxic productivity at the start of this book and it's important to mention it again here. Toxic productivity is the unhealthy desire to be productive at all times, at all costs. That desire to go the 'extra mile' is not unique to employees, and when you're working for yourself, it's something you'll need to watch out for. I have a tendency to run and run, working harder and harder and then I stop to take time off. I used to tell myself I was bored or ready for a change, but the truth is that I was burning myself out, over and over again.

Think about how many clients you actually want to work with. Nancy told me that she's very conscious of not taking on too much work. 'I don't want to fall into this trap of having to say yes to everything because that wasn't part of the vision or the purpose.'

I meet many people who, like me, work very hard because they love what they do, and they feel a great sense of urgency to help as many people as they can. Francis told me he's driven to protect as many people as he can from cyber-hacking. 'When you love what you do, it doesn't feel like work. Sometimes I wish my weeks were longer.' I know exactly what he means. It often feels like I don't have enough time to achieve everything I want to, to help as many people as I can make the right decisions for them and their lives.

The truth is that you can't go full throttle all the time. Running a business is a marathon not a sprint. I've learned over the years that balance is key – between work, however much I love it, and fun. Between working hard and looking after my mental and physical health. Health is everything. My business has to fit around my health rather than the other way around.

It will take you time to figure out what works for you. Allow yourself that time and be patient with yourself. You will learn so much about yourself through this process. Some things may be difficult to accept; others will be pleasant surprises. It can feel like a rollercoaster ride. The best strategy is to take it one step at a time.

CHAPTER 17

You're On Your Way

'Believe in yourself. You are braver than you think, more talented than you know, and capable of more than you can imagine.'
— Roy T Bennett, author[27]

When I decided to leave contracting, there were many people who thought I was crazy – 'Small business owners don't have any money, Lisa. This is a crazy move!' I was earning a lot of money in a job that I loved. But I wanted more freedom. I wanted to be able to serve more people and see what I could achieve.

There's an element of having to trust yourself and trust the process. You're not really going to know what it feels like until you're on the other side. For

---

27 RT Bennett, *The Light in the Heart: Inspirational thoughts for living your best life* (Roy Bennett, 2020)

Nancy, her first few months were about 'getting some real belief that this could be a business that's bigger than just me.' Another interviewee described it as 'an exploration and an opportunity to learn some things about myself that I can take forward.'

For me, running my own business means I can manage my own life. It's about freedom and control and having choices. 'My time is my own,' Justin told me. 'I listen to the universe talking to me, letting me know when to stop and be at one with what is. I have built the capacity to be able to tune into what my needs are in the moment and to be able to act on them spontaneously and creatively.'

When we're facing challenges, it's easy to feel lonely, so it's important to connect with like-minded people along the way. We've talked about networking from a business development perspective, but don't underestimate its value in terms of keeping you sane. Caroline joined a business networking group early on and found it invaluable. 'There were lots of people like me, who were struggling with the same things as me, were happy to help and offer me impartial advice.'

Managing your own time is a huge bonus. Although Sophie works long hours, she's able to structure her work in ways that mean she can spend time with her family and manage the ebbs and flows of her business. She told me that when she was in full-time employment, she always felt guilty if she had a dentist appointment. She felt people were looking at her wondering if she was going to an interview. 'If I'm sick, don't pay me! I don't need the politics in my life!'

One of the things that takes people by surprise is how efficient you can be when you manage your own time. 'It's not a badge of honour to work every hour and be exhausted!' one interviewee told me. 'It's absolutely wonderful to discover that I can add more value to the world in half the number of hours and still have time to walk the dog, simply by not being part of a corporate machine or building something for someone else.'

For Nancy, the control and the freedom have been life-changing. 'My brain hadn't thought for a very long time,' she told me. 'It had made decisions in high-pressured situations, but it had not had the time to really think.' She described how her daily walk has become a non-negotiable for her. She's realised that being able to really think is a skill in itself. 'I can read documents for hours sitting at my desk, and the answer will come when I'm walking around the meadows near where I live.' Having the freedom to think has been 'lovely and really, really refreshing.'

For some, the reality of no longer being in the corporate environment is a huge relief. Sophie told me that for her, the best thing is the lack of politics. 'When you're advising a client, you're external, so they'll take what you're saying on face value. You don't have an angle!'

Instead of struggling to manage upwards, Andy told me, 'When the idiot in charge starts making decisions, I can have a conversation with myself about it.' He enjoys the fact that he has nobody else to blame but himself. He's in charge of his own decisions. 'If somebody has made a dumb decision in the company, it's either been made by me, or somebody I made a dumb decision to employ, or somebody I made a dumb decision to ask to do something with the information and resources I gave them. The buck stops with me.'

Ultimately, this choice is about doing things your way – to quote Tamara, 'the freedom and flexibility to be able to make my own rules, to make my life work for me.'

What if it doesn't work?

Running your own business is not for everyone. There may come a time when your priorities change, or you realise that this life isn't working for you.

I've worked with a few people who've tried the entrepreneurial life and it hasn't worked for them. What they had in common was a sense of guilt and shame about this, which I've encouraged them to overcome. There is no shame in trying something and failing.

There should be no guilt in choosing to prioritise your own mental health or the financial stability of your family.

It's easy to get caught up in the entrepreneurial cachet. Anish told me he was going back through some of his journals and laughing at what he chose to prioritise when he started his business. 'I had this matrix which showed effort versus value. Low effort, high value was getting a job and I just dismissed it. I was so invested in this.' He made the decision to return to paid employment to stabilise his family finances. He has two young children and his wife's business is taking off and requires support.

Nothing is forever, and life is all about choices. What I will tell you is that having run your own business, your life will never be the same. You will always carry that experience with you wherever you go. You may well view any future employer as a client, as part of your portfolio. You're likely to retain an entrepreneurial mindset and be much more open to the opportunities that life presents.

Conclusion

'Being kind to yourself only when you deserve it is like watering a plant only when it rains.'
— Unknown

I've laid out in this book the key elements that I and the many others I've worked with considered as they made the transition from employment to running their own businesses. I've shared with you the lessons I've learned and am still learning, in the hopes that you can avoid some of the mistakes I made along the way.

I remember hearing a speaker and author of several great books on entrepreneurship talk about discovering what you want to do with your life. He spoke about looking back and seeing 'the thread' that weaves throughout your life, maybe all the way back to your childhood: the successes and failures, those moments that stay with you, the memories and experiences that have brought you to where you are today. Often, we don't understand why we've made certain choices in our lives, why certain things happen, until one day it all comes together, and we can look back and understand why we find ourselves where we are today. You are exactly where you need to be and who you need to be. Right here, right now.

We all have our ups and downs. It's tough to keep showing up every day, to keep doing the work, to keep believing in yourself. When times are tough or I'm having a wobble, I keep my head down and focus on today and tomorrow, doing the work and getting things done. When I'm feeling confident and happy, I lift my head up and consider the months and years ahead. I allow myself to tweak things. I look at options, set goals and make decisions.

Being hard on yourself is a complete waste of time and energy. We're all creatures of emotion and our feelings are never static. Whatever your reality this morning, later on today, over the weekend, it's different from the experience of next week or next month. We all have cycles and rhythms. We all have our own individual triggers, hopes and fears. The tapestry of our lives is made up of a myriad of experiences, thoughts and feelings.

Most of us have internalised a lot of perfectionism. Without realising it consciously, we hold ourselves to ridiculously high standards that are not helpful. We worry that if we cut ourselves some slack, we're lazy. Our fear is that terrible things will happen to us if we don't continue to hustle all day, every day.

There's a saying that when life gives you lemons, you should make lemonade. But the truth is that it's hard to make lemonade when you're dealing with the impact of the lemons. You know what's worse than feeling exhausted? Feeling exhausted and also guilty about not being more productive. Being kind and compassionate to yourself is not being soft or weak or lowering your standards. It's the best way to help yourself move forward. Watch your language. 'Shoulds' are not helpful.

There's no doubt that this is a big step you're taking, but you're not doing it alone. There are people in your corner, people who want you to succeed, who are there to support you. Your accountant, your virtual assistant, the person who designs your website. And me. The reason I wrote this book is because I want to support your journey. I want to give you the confidence to back yourself.

Above all, this is a creative process and an emotional one. Give yourself the time and space you need to design the life you deserve. Be kind to yourself and please ask for help. That's what I'm here for. I believe in you.

Acknowledgements

When I started my coaching business, I focused my efforts on helping business owners. I knew I had the skills and experience to help them simplify, grow and enjoy their businesses. During the writing of my first book, *The REAL Entrepreneur*, I didn't feel that my own story, how I transitioned from the corporate world to starting my various businesses, was relevant to the people I was writing for.

In January 2020, I was conducting a coaching session with a CEO client and her COO. There'd been a mix-up with room bookings, so we were having our conversation in the lounge of a London club I was a member of. As we stood up to say our goodbyes at the end of the session, a lady who'd been sitting nearby spoke up. 'Are you a coach?' she asked. I was so focused on my clients I'm not sure I even answered her. Instead, my client told her I was an excellent coach and that she should take my card. On the call that followed, Nancy explained that she was looking for support in navigating the politics of her current role and advice on how to handle certain situations at work. I explained that I was a business coach and worked with entrepreneurs and their teams. 'But you're a coach, right?' she insisted. 'I feel strongly that I want to be coached by you.'

Working with Nancy brought back a lot of memories for me about my time in the corporate world – the emotions she was describing, the situations she was encountering. She told me that she'd tried going freelance before but it hadn't worked for her, so she was determined to make her career work in employment. I would never try to influence anyone to follow the path I took – leaving a well-paid job to venture out on my own. But as Nancy and I worked together, she kept returning to the idea of building the life that she wanted and doing things her way.

As with so many people, the pandemic enabled her to take a step back and look at her life through new eyes, and working with her did the same for me. In April 2021 she left employment and started her own business and in that same month, I decided I had to write this book.

More and more clients have been finding their way to me, despite the fact that my online presence makes it clear that I work with people who already run their own businesses. People who want my help in deciding whether running their own business is right for them. But the very first was Nancy and I'm hugely grateful to her for being so sure that I was the right coach for her. She shows up, does the work and faces her fears every day. I am so proud of what she's achieving and who she's allowing herself to be. To benefit from coaching requires honesty and I'm grateful to everyone who is willing to go there with me.

Many people have helped with the creation of this book, but special mention must go to those people who gave generously of their time to be interviewed: Andy Pieroux, Anish Hindocha, Austin Peat, Caroline Somer, Didrik Skantze, Francis West, Justin Lee, Katy Hampton, Nancy Lamb, Sophie Wright and Tamara Makoni. Many others agreed for their experiences to be shared anonymously. I am grateful for their insights and perspectives. I also had the benefit of feedback from some great beta readers, with special thanks going to Austin, Kat, Isobel, Andy and Tamara for their thorough review and honest critique.

No book gets published without a team of people bringing it all together. Once again, the team at Rethink Press made the process painless. I cannot recommend them highly enough.

My husband and I have been together fifteen years. Like most couples, we've had our fair share of ups and downs and he hasn't always been able to understand why I do what I do. But when I told him I was thinking of writing a second book, his immediate reaction was: 'If you've got a second book in you, then you must write it.' It's been an incredibly challenging nine months as our businesses continue to grow and we take further steps to build the life we want, but never once has he swayed from his conviction that this book needed to be written. I thank him for all the many ways in which he sees me for who I am and supports the path I have chosen. I can't imagine being on this wonderful journey of life with anyone else.

Leaving employment is not for everyone. For me the decision was life-changing, and something I've never once regretted. Having the freedom and flexibility to build my life my way is all I've ever wanted. It's hard work but it's also a huge privilege. I believe that each of us deserves to love what we do. There has never been a better time to get really clear about how you want your life to be, what's going to work for you and how to do things your way. I hope this book has helped you on your path.

The Author

Lisa Zevi is an operational business coach, TEDx speaker and author of the Amazon Number 1 bestselling book *The REAL Entrepreneur: How to simplify, grow and enjoy your business.*

She has been building productive teams, driving change and helping people get organised for twenty-five years, working in multinational corporates and investment banks before starting her own coaching business in 2017. She has extensive experience of hiring, managing and retaining great people and now works with business owners of fast-growing small businesses, helping them free up their time, scale their operations, get out of the day-to-day and build strong, inclusive teams.

Lisa runs an online community of entrepreneurs from all over the world – The REAL Entrepreneurs Community – where small business owners collaborate, share and learn.

She is passionate about empowering women and helping them achieve greater confidence and self-awareness. She believes that each of us deserves to love what we do.

🌐 www.lisazevi.com

🔗 https://linktr.ee/lisazevi